WEATHER

·

JOHN FARRAND, JR.

·

STEWART, TABORI & CHANG
NEW YORK

·

Cover:
Rain storm in Monument Valley, Utah.

Back cover:
Cloud spilling over Continental Divide, Glacier National Park.

Half-title:
Frost on window at sunrise, Virginia.

Pages 2–3:
Wind-etched ripple marks in sand, Eureka Sand Dunes, California.

Pages 4–5:
Geysers in the cold air of Iceland.

Page 6:
Cumulus clouds over Utah.

Title page:
Ice-coated lighthouse on Lake Michigan.

Page 9:
Light rain in New York's Times Square, 1943.

Page 10:
The effects of a hurricane in Galveston, Texas.

Pages 12–13:
Lightning, Phoenix, Arizona.

Pages 14–15:
Storm clouds over Glacier National Park, Montana.

Text copyright © 1990 John Farrand, Jr.
Picture credits appear on pages 238–239.

Published in 1990 by
Stewart, Tabori & Chang, Inc.
575 Broadway, New York, New York 10012

Distributed in the U.S. by Workman Publishing,
708 Broadway, New York, New York 10003

Distributed in Canada by Canadian Manda Group,
P.O. Box 920 Station U, Toronto, Ontario M8Z 5P9

Distributed in all other territories by Little,
Brown and Company, International Division, 34 Beacon Street,
Boston, Massachusetts 02108

Printed in Japan

10 9 8 7 6 5 4 3 2 1

Library of Congress Cataloging-in-Publication Data

Farrand, John.
    Weather / by John Farrand, Jr.
        p.   cm.
    ISBN 1-55670-134-9 : $35.00
    1. Weather—Popular works. I. Title.
QC981.2.F37   1988
551.5—dc20   89-28595
                                           CIP

CONTENTS

FOREWORD

"IT IS RAINING." "IT IS COLD." STATEMENTS SUCH AS THESE, which have equivalents in many languages, are an indication of how important the weather is in our lives. Almost alone among English words, the weather is "It." Our daily speech contains dozens of metaphors that reveal that the weather is never far from our thoughts. One can be snowed in, dewy-eyed, under a cloud, in a fog, or in the doldrums, have a sunny outlook, be caught up in a whirlwind of activity, engage in a heated argument, rain on someone's parade, and receive a shower of congratulations, a deluge of mail, a cold reception, a storm of protest, or warm praise. One's facial expression or disposition can be icy, frozen, frosty, frigid, cold, chilly, or misty. Turning the tables, we say that the weather is gloomy, sultry, brisk, or dreary.

These expressions are more than just figures of speech. The weather is known to affect how we feel. It is perhaps no accident that both a low-pressure sys-tem and a feeling of sadness are called a "depression." Or that a feeling of well-being is called a "high." Weather influences our lives in other ways. In everything from planning picnics to harvesting crops, from deciding what one should wear to whether commercial fishing fleets put out to sea, from postponing golf games to scheduling space flights, weather alters our lives.

Weather affects the lives of animals and plants as well, and it was this that first sparked my interest in the weather. As a beginning naturalist, I soon realized that what I would discover on an excursion, and what I would find it doing, depended on the weather. If the wind was out of the south on an autumn day, I knew there would be no migrating birds. When a period of drought was followed by rain, I knew that on the first sunny day after that I would find lots of fresh but-terflies that had needed the moisture to emerge. When the wind shifted to the northwest after a late-

A winter snowstorm adds to the beauty of Washington State's Olympic National Park.

summer period of rain, I knew the air would be full of thistledown, because these plants wait for dry air to arrive before sending forth their seeds. If the sky was cloudy, I learned that I would see no dragonflies over the local pond, because they need sunlight to warm their flight muscles; if I returned to the same pond an hour later when the sun was shining, the air would be full of dragonflies skimming over the water.

So I began to take notes on the weather on days when I was going into the field. Soon a pattern began to emerge. Air masses moved through my area and I could predict whether the air they brought with them would be colder or warmer by the clouds that accompanied them. Approaching low-pressure systems could be detected long before they arrived. Then, when I watched a hurricane begin to come ashore in Louisiana and saw the great banks of clouds spinning counterclockwise, as clouds do around all cyclones in the northern hemisphere, I was hooked. The weather was as interesting as the animals and plants that had enticed me into the open in the first place.

This book is the result of my explorations into the world of the weather. Many have helped me to write it. David M. Ludlum, the most weather-wise person I know, gave the manuscript a thorough and critical reading. Daril Bentley, Peter F. Cannell, G. Stuart Keith, Kenneth K. Tate, Alan Weissman, and Ann H. Whitman made valuable suggestions or provided useful information. Jose Pouso and Sarah Longacre performed extensive research on the illustrations and assisted in selecting them. My editor, Brian D. Hotchkiss, was enthusiastic and encouraging as he both followed the course of the book and guided the path it took. I am deeply grateful to all of them for their assistance, and must add that any errors of fact or interpretation are my own.

In 1735, Benjamin Franklin wrote: "Some are weather-wise, some are otherwise." I hope this book will help to put you in the former category.

The heavy bands with dark undersides help distinguish these altocumulus clouds from the higher and more delicate-looking cirrocumulus.

(PAGES 20–21): Despite the usual heat, night temperatures in deserts often drop low enough to permit frost to form, as here in the Chisos Mountains of Texas.

CHAPTER 1
FROM GODS TO SATELLITES: EXPLAINING THE WEATHER

ACCORDING TO THE DAKOTA, NOMADIC BUFFALO HUNTERS who lived on the northern Great Plains of North America, the four Wakinyan—the Thunderbirds—dwelled in the Black Hills. They were concealed by dark clouds and could not be seen, but their voice was thunder and their symbol was forked lightning. Like the motion of a cyclone, their movements were counterclockwise, whereas the motion of all other things in nature was clockwise. In the earliest times, the Thunderbirds fought a long struggle for control of the earth with Unktehi, the Water Monster and bringer of floods. This destructive battle was a stalemate until Wakinyan Tanka, the Great Thunderbird of the West, robed in black, summoned the other Wakinyan to their mountaintop home, where they decided that their proper domain was the sky and the air. The Thunderbirds withdrew into the sky and in a final attempt to defeat Unktehi let loose all their fury.

In this last holocaust, Unktehi was burned up. (Her bones are visible to this day as the Badlands.) The few humans who had survived came out of hiding, and peace reigned at last. Already in control of thunder, fire, and wind, the four Wakinyan had now acquired power over water. They became benevolent spirits who, although they cause severe storms, provide all that is life-giving and cleansing in the weather.

This ancient tale, like similar accounts throughout the world, embodied and explained everything that could be observed about the weather. A passage from the Book of Job, probably written in the fifth century B.C., contains a strikingly similar image:

And now men see not the bright light which is in the clouds: but the wind passeth, and cleanseth them.

Fair weather cometh out of the north: with God is terrible majesty.

The Israelites, too, had a cosmology that encompassed the weather, as did all of the great civilizations of antiquity—in China, in India, along the Tigris and

Horses on a hilltop in South Dakota, under the cloudless sky of a Polar Continental air mass.

(PAGES 24–25): According to the ancient tale, the Badlands of South Dakota are the parched bones of Unktehi, the Water Monster.

(PAGES 26–27): As a rainstorm sweeps over Sleeping Ute Mountain in Colorado, it is easy to imagine that its curving sheets of rain are the robes of an unseen Thunderbird.

Euphrates, and in Egypt. All had systems of belief in which weather was under the control of the gods, although they also had more earthly proverbs like Job's "Fair weather cometh out of the north."

The Greeks were the first to attempt an explanation of the weather that relied entirely on physical science, rather than on a traditional cosmology. In the seventh century B.C., Thales of Miletus tried to associate weather with the movement of heavenly bodies, and considered water to be the basic element of all matter. He knew that water rises from the earth and then descends from the sky, but he didn't understand the process of condensation or the nature of clouds. His student Anaximander understood that wind was moving air, an idea that was rejected by other Greek philosophers, including Aristotle.

In the fifth century B.C., Anaxagoras was correct in noting that in hot, summer weather water rose to great heights, where it froze into hailstones. Similarly, he proposed that rain formed when clouds rose to cold altitudes, where their moisture condensed. But he thought that beyond this cold upper atmosphere was a zone composed of a firelike substance he called aether. It was this aether, trapped in clouds, that caused thunder and lightning. For Anaxagoras, water was not the basic element of matter; instead, matter was composed of an infinite number of particles, each with its own unique qualities.

The most important Greek natural philosopher before Aristotle was Empedocles, who proposed in the fifth century B.C. that there were four basic elements rather than one or an infinite number. The four ele-

ments of Empedocles were earth, air, fire, and water. Fire and water were antagonistic, since water quenches a fire, but earth and air had an affinity for one another. This opposition and affinity governed the four qualities of heat, cold, moistness, and dryness. Empedocles tried to use these basic elements and their interactions to explain the seasons. Despite the fact that his four elements moved about randomly and not regularly, he proposed that when fire was dominant, the weather was warm and summery, but when water dominated, winter weather prevailed.

These systems contained both kernels of truth and shortcomings, and they all influenced the greatest of the Greek scientists, Aristotle. Written about 340 B.C., Aristotle's *Meteorologica* was the first lengthy and comprehensive treatment of the weather. Aristotle regarded the universe as spherical, composed of concentric layers with the earth at their center. The outer layers, beyond the orbit of the moon, were the realm of the planets and stars, and Aristotle identified these layers as the province of astronomy. What happened in the inner layers was the domain of meteorology.

In describing and explaining the inner layers—the terrestrial region—Aristotle adopted Empedocles' notion of four elements and arranged them in layers. The outermost layer was composed of fire, beneath this layer was air, and beneath that, water. At the center was earth, the fourth element. Although he arranged them in discrete layers, Aristotle realized that the four elements could mingle: Fires could burn on earth, and land rose above the water. Moreover, he held that the elements were interchangeable; heat could cause water to evaporate, changing it into a

As a thunderstorm moves over Tucson, Arizona, brilliant bolts of lightning dart both from clouds to ground and from cloud to cloud.

29

moist substance similar to air. This moist substance, though not water, gave rise to clouds and rain, while another of his "exhalations," hot and dry, was the cause of winds and thunder. Aristotle theorized that clouds could not form above the tops of mountains because this was in the layer of fire, too hot for condensation to occur. For the same reason, he disagreed with the explanation of hail proposed by Anaxagoras; these upper reaches were too hot for hailstones to form. Instead, he proposed that large droplets of water were suspended in the air and that these could only freeze into hailstones in cold air close to the ground. He also denied that rain resulted from the ascent of clouds; precipitation too could only occur close to the ground, safely removed from the enclosing layer of fire.

It turns out that Aristotle was wrong about the formation of hailstones and rain and that Anaxagoras was right. The reason for these and other errors of Aristotle's can be found in the difference between his

In the wake of a front moving away to the left, ragged cumulus clouds herald the return of clear weather at Stonehenge, the megalithic ring of great stones on the Salisbury Plain in southern England.

scientific method and that of the earlier natural philosophers, and in the difference between Greek science and the methods used in science today. Thales, Anaximander, Anaxagoras, and Empedocles, using the inductive method, all began with direct observations and then tried to explain them on the basis of what they observed. Aristotle, although a tireless and keen observer who probed into most aspects of natural science, did things the other way around, using the deductive method. He began with an all-encompassing view of the universe and tried to fit the weather phenomena into his preconceived system.

Despite its errors, Aristotle's *Meteorologica* was the most successful of the classical attempts to explain the weather, precisely because he had prepared a structured view of the universe that enabled him to attempt a systematic discussion of all aspects of weather. Aristotle, with his deductions about the weather based on a comprehensible picture of the universe, was not the first to study the weather and

A sandstorm moves among the tall mesas of Monument Valley in Arizona. Although these rock formations were carved from the Colorado Plateau by ancient rivers, they have been polished and shaped by windblown sand.

attempt to explain it, but he is regarded as the founder of the science of meteorology because he carried the ancient methods as far as they could be taken. For nearly 2,000 years, no one was in a position to add anything significant to what he had proposed, or to present convincing alternatives to his ideas. He remained the final authority on the subject until the Renaissance, when his deductive approach and the inductive method of his predecessors were supplemented by a different scientific method, one seldom used and all but impossible in classical Greece.

The new approach was the experimental method, in which ideas are tested by carefully designed experiments. Regardless of preconceived systems, the truth of a scientific assertion is now judged by the results of experiments, rather than by observations alone. Even the most elaborate system can collapse if a single experiment fails to support it. The experimental method became possible only with the development of precision instruments for measuring and recording information. As soon as such instruments started to appear, meteorology and other sciences began to move forward again. Despite the fact that most

scientific research was done in libraries rather than in laboratories, dogma could not withstand the steady accumulation of experimental evidence and of precise data gathered with newly invented instruments.

Some of the ancient Greeks had held that even when water evaporated it was still water, in the form of a vapor. Aristotle himself had realized that at least some of his warm, moist exhalation produced rain. The first important meteorological device was a simple one used to measure the humidity of the atmosphere. It was developed by the German mathematician Nicholas de Cusa, who in the fifteenth century hung out some wool and noted that it was heavier when moisture in the air had condensed onto it. More sophisticated instruments were developed as centuries passed. One of these was a hanging cord of twisted catgut with a metal arrow attached to its free end; as the cord picked up or lost moisture, its coil tightened or loosened, causing the arrow to turn along a dial. This instrument was invented in 1768 by Johann Heinrich Lambert, the German physicist who also coined the term *hygrometer*.

Although it had been known in ancient times that gases and liq-

As a storm cloud moves over the New Zealand countryside, rain falls from the cloud's darkened underside. Sunlight reflected from droplets of mist often produces rainbows, such as this one in the misty "cloud forest" of the Vilcabamba Mountains of southern Peru (OPPOSITE), and another in Alaska's Lake Clark National Park (PAGES 36–37).

(PAGES 34–35): **A crashing surf on Lake Michigan attests to the power of the wind.**

uids expand when heated, Galileo was the first to realize that this fact provides a means of measuring temperature. In Padua, probably in 1593, he invented the first thermometer—a simple glass tube with a bulb at one end. After heating the bulb in his hand, Galileo placed the open end of the tube in a dish of water. As the bulb cooled, the air in the bulb contracted, drawing water up into the tube, on which Galileo had scratched marks to indicate the change in temperature. This simple device was quickly copied and refined by scientists in several countries; precise and comparable measurement of temperature became standard. It was now possible to record temperatures at different times and in different places, and a flurry of experiments and refinements followed. In 1701, Isaac Newton fixed the freezing point of water at zero "degrees of heat." Using mercury instead of water, the German physicist Gabriel Fahrenheit developed his scale in 1714; the Swedish astronomer Anders Celsius proposed his in 1736.

As a full moon sets over Sitka Sound in southeast Alaska, advection fog rolls in from the Pacific Ocean.

(PAGES 38–39): A winter ground fog has given a coat of frost to the branches of cottonwood trees near Bear Lake in northern Utah.

The barometer was another important invention. Aristotle had proved that air was a substance by pointing out that it had to be emptied out of a vessel before the vessel could be filled with water. But because a leather bag had the same weight when full of air as when flattened out, he concluded that air was weightless. In 1643, the Florentine mathematician Evangelista Torricelli took a glass tube that was open at one end and expanded into a bulb at the other, and inserted the open end into a dish of water. As he watched the water rise and fall in the tube, he concluded that these changes were caused by variations in the weight of air pushing down on the water in the dish, with a heavier layer of air forcing more of the water up into the tube. Because his water barometer had to be sixty feet tall to record these changes, Torricelli switched to mercury, which is much heavier than water. This enabled him to use a tube only 32 inches tall, a type of barometer still used today. A variety of other barometers, including the aneroid barometer, were invented later, giving rise to another proliferation of experiments and measurements followed.

Other instruments, such as wind gauges and calibrated rain gauges, were invented during this same period, and the stage was set for the next phase in the history of weather science, in which the properties of water and air were verified by experiments, and large-scale, systematic gathering of precise weather measurements and observations began.

Drawing on this large body of information, scientists were now in a position to try to explain the motion of the atmosphere. The first such attempt was that of Edmund Halley, an English astronomer who is most famous for predicting the return of the comet that now bears his name. In 1686, Halley published a paper in which he proposed that air heated by the sun rises and that winds are caused by air flowing in to replace air that has risen. The constant rising of heated air keeps the atmosphere in a continuous state of motion, as air moves toward areas that are heated. Halley's concept was refined during the next centuries. There gradually emerged a picture in which air rose at the Equator, flowed northward and southward, cooled, and then sank back to the surface. A pattern of global atmospheric circulation had begun to emerge.

On Michigan's Upper Peninsula, an autumn frost has edged the red and green leaves of wild strawberries.

On October 21, 1743, an eclipse of the moon occurred that was visible in eastern North America. Benjamin Franklin had hoped to witness it in Philadelphia, but the eclipse was obscured by a storm. A few days later he received a letter from his brother, who had seen the eclipse in Boston because the sky there was clear; his brother happened to add that a storm had occurred in Boston on the following day. This fact caused Franklin to speculate that the storm in Philadelphia and the one in Boston were the same, and that this single storm had traveled northeast from Philadelphia to Boston. He therefore proposed the idea of the motion of storms.

A problem with Franklin's notion, one that he never fully resolved, was that on the night of the storm in Philadelphia, the wind had been out of the northeast, blowing in exactly the opposite direction from that which one would expect if the storm were moving toward Boston. The resolution of this apparent contradiction began in 1821, after a September hurricane moved through southern New England. William Redfield of Cromwell, Connecticut, walked across Connecticut, Rhode Island, and Massachusetts, plotting the positions of trees that had fallen during the hurricane. In 1831, after much study, Redfield proposed the theory of circular winds in storms, noting that the pattern of fallen trees he had observed could only be explained if the storm had been a giant whirlwind. As Franklin's storm had moved over Philadelphia, he had recorded a northeasterly wind that was part of a circular flow around the center of the storm. Today this circulation is termed cyclonic, and such a storm is called a cyclone. Another American, James Espy, disagreed with Redfield's concept, and proposed instead that air moved straight inward toward the center of a storm because this was a region of low atmospheric pressure, and that the air then rose as a result of heating until it cooled, causing its moisture to condense and form clouds and rain. This, according to Espy, was the cause of such storms. As it turned out, the ideas of both Redfield and Espy were partly correct.

In 1918, the Norwegian physicist Vilhelm Bjerknes and his son Jacob discovered that many weather phenomena result from the meeting and interaction of warm and cold masses of air. Their proposal associated air masses, fronts, and the formation of cyclones. In 1939, Carl-Gustaf Rossby, working for the United States Weather Bureau, discovered the mid-latitude jet stream in the northern hemisphere, which travels eastward at an altitude of about 30,000 to 40,000 feet and governs the easterly movement of much of our weather. With this discovery, the modern concept of the circulation of the atmosphere had become essentially complete.

Today, with high-altitude balloons, radar, satellites, and advanced computers, the movements and behavior of the atmosphere can be plotted with considerable precision, and weather forecasts can be made with an ever-increasing degree of accuracy.

Our present understanding of how weather works is very different from the beliefs of the tribes that once hunted on the Great Plains. But the weather is no less majestic than the cloud-robed Wakinyan, whose thunder still rumbles out of the Black Hills of South Dakota.

The great volcanic cone of Mount Edgecumbe looms in the distance beyond fog-shrouded Sitka Sound.

CHAPTER 2
THE VAST AND WANDERING AIR: AIR MASSES

DRIVEN BY FORCES DERIVED FROM THE ROTATION OF THE earth and by atmospheric pressure differences, cool, damp air slides from the North Pacific onto the fog-drenched, rocky shores of British Columbia and southern Alaska. As the misty oceanic air climbs the slopes of the mountains along the coast, it sheds much of its moisture as rain—frequent showers that sustain some of the richest and most luxuriant forests in all of the northern hemisphere, the great tract of giant conifers along the Northwest Coast of North America.

After crossing several more mountain ranges, each time losing more moisture, the Pacific air spills down the easternmost slopes of the Rockies and spreads out over the broad lands beyond. Here, sheltered from the wind in the lee of the mountains it has just crossed, the air begins to accumulate over the lowlands, and soon a huge dome of air builds up, covering hundreds of thousands or even millions of square miles. As this dome grows, the current of air that feeds it gradually slows, and finally wanes to nothing. The dome becomes a vast, motionless reservoir of air several miles thick.

What, exactly, drives the westerly winds that have brought air from the Pacific Ocean to the dry interior of Canada? As the earth slowly rotates from west to east on its axis, any object traveling away from the Equator, even a bullet fired from a rifle, is deflected eastward in both the northern and the southern hemispheres. Solar radiation beating down on the region around the Equator causes air to warm and rise and to flow toward the poles. The earth's rotational force, called the Coriolis force, causes the flow of air to curve gradually to the east, and by the time the stream of air has reached 30 degrees North latitude—about the level of Houston, Cairo, New Delhi, and Shanghai in the northern hemisphere—where the air was once moving toward the North Pole, it is now flowing due northeast. It has become a powerful and constant southwest-to-northeast current of air in the mid-latitudes of the northern hemisphere. Called the west-

A high-pressure system lies over White River National Forest in Colorado (OPPOSITE), bringing clear, crisp, and still air to these rugged mountains.

(PAGES 46–47): Moist and cloud-filled air, fresh from the Pacific Ocean, flows eastward over the crest of the Cascade Range in Oregon, shedding its rain. Before this air reaches the interior lowlands, it will be clear and dry.

erly jet stream, it flows at an altitude of about eight miles above the surface, with an average speed of 100 miles an hour, although speeds of more than 800 miles an hour have been measured. A similar jet stream flows eastward in the southern hemisphere. These great winds steer all but the largest and strongest weather systems in a generally eastward direction. It is the force of the northern jet stream, powered ultimately by the heat of the sun, that brings air eastward from the Pacific Ocean, and which drives air from the North Atlantic ashore in Europe.

Another pair of jet streams, the subtropical, flow at about 30 degrees latitude. Their flow is weaker than that of the northern jet streams. The subtropical jet streams separate warm tropical air from the cooler air to the north and south.

In the northern hemisphere, continents alter the even flow of westerly air streams, and local conditions can bend the air, or, as in the case of air lying to the east of the Rocky Mountains, interrupt the flow altogether. At these same latitudes in the southern hemisphere, there is more ocean than land, and one result is the Roaring Forties, where sea winds blow almost continuously and unimpeded from the west. Sailors have always taken advantage of these rough but dependable winds to travel quickly around the world in the southern oceans. Magellan, it turns out, went the wrong way, against the wind.

Like all stalled domes of air in the northern hemisphere, the Canadian dome responds to these same forces by slowly spinning clockwise around its center. (Similar domes of air in the southern hemisphere spin counterclockwise). Beneath it lies the vast, flat interior of Canada, a region of prairies, grassy marshes, trackless forests, and cold lakes and rivers that stretches from the base of the Rockies to the Atlantic Ocean. A dome of air can lie here for days or even weeks, while the immense Canadian landscape, dry and cold, gradually imparts its character to the air above it. Once a stream of air fresh from the ocean, cool and damp, it is now cold, dry, and clear. During its long rest, this large dome of atmosphere takes on a flavor all its own. The current of air has now become an air mass, a more or less stationary accumulation of air. Born in the cold interior of Canada, this particular air mass is called the Polar Continental, one of the twenty or so air masses in the world.

The air has gathered into an enormous, invisible dome, whose center—where the "pile" of air is deeper—weighs more than its thinner edges. This weight, known as barometric pressure, gives the air mass a certain physical strength. Barometric pressure at the dome's center is high, explaining why one of these air masses is often called a high, or a high-pressure system. An air mass is also called an anti-cyclone because air flows around it in the opposite direction from that of a storm system, or cyclone. Air masses often grow quite large, their very weight forc-

(OPPOSITE): As a dome of cold autumn air lies over Glacier National Park, a light wind lifts the air high enough for a small wave cloud to form in an otherwise clear sky.

(PAGES 50–51): This arid, grassy landscape in Saskatchewan lies in the "rain shadow" of the Canadian Rockies. Any Pacific air that reaches it will have long since lost its moisture in the mountains.

ing smaller air masses to move around them; storms, unless they themselves are very large, cannot interfere with large air masses. Thus, the weather inside one of these giant, sweeping anticyclones tends to remain clear, and is more apt to influence the behavior of other weather systems than they are to influence it.

At any given moment, much of the air in our atmosphere is flowing toward the east, but here and there some is gathered in great, gently spinning air masses. Some, such as the Polar Continental, are centered over continents, while others form over relatively warm portions of the ocean. Continental air masses tend to be cold and dry, while those that originate over the ocean are warmer and more laden with moisture. A third type, the Arctic air mass, forms in the polar regions; its frigid and very dry air rarely spills southward into the temperate zone.

Although these high-pressure systems cause changes in the weather, a newly formed Polar Continental air mass will have little impact on weather anywhere else as long as it remains stalled over Canada. And it may well remain stalled here for days, particularly in winter. But sooner or later, pushed by the westerly flow, the air mass will break out of its sheltered place of origin and begin to move. Like all anticyclones in the northern hemisphere, Polar Continental air moves to the east and south. Those in the southern hemisphere travel to the east and north. The air of a Polar Continental high is almost always drier and colder than the air lying to its south. Most of the time, the weather produced by a Polar Continental anticyclone is crisp and clean, with skies that are cloudless or dotted with puffy little cumulus clouds.

Exactly what happens when Polar Continental air spills out of Canada depends on where it goes. Should it enter the northeastern United States, existing humid air or rain will give way to the Polar Continental's clear skies and cool, northwest winds, which sometimes even bear the scent of the spruces and firs of its birthplace. Air flowing down over the Great Lakes in winter picks up moisture again, and, if the lakes are not frozen, high clouds and snow flurries develop. If this same air crosses the Great Lakes and then moves on eastward over the Appalachians, another round of snow flurries may fall in the mountains before the high moves on into New England or across the Atlantic coastal plain.

When Polar Continental air spreads southward toward the Gulf of Mexico, as sometimes happens, it is trespassing on the territory of warm, moist air masses from the tropical seas. Heavy showers are likely to develop when these two very different air masses confront each other. On rare occasions in winter, Polar Continental air slides to the southwest, down over the Great Plains, across the Rocky Mountains and Sierra Nevada, and eventually to the coast of California. Because it has encountered no open water during this long, southward journey, the air is still dry and very cold. The arrival of Polar Continental air—and thus sudden, freezing temperatures—on the balmy coast of southern California can spell disaster for agriculture, often meaning higher prices nationwide for citrus fruits and other warm-weather crops.

The Polar Continental is one of three air masses important in the weather in North America east of the

Slowly dissipating in the sky above Glacier National Park, the contrails of passing jetliners indicate that there is more moisture at these altitudes than is apparent from the ground.

Rocky Mountains. The other two are the Tropical Gulf and the Tropical Atlantic. Tropical Gulf and Tropical Atlantic highs develop over the calm waters south of the United States, providing the warm and pleasant weather that attracts thousands of tourists to the Caribbean every year. But when such moisture-laden, tropical air pushes northward over land in winter, the result is clouds, drizzle, and sometimes nighttime fog.

In summer, these two oceanic air masses behave somewhat differently when they come ashore in the United States. Both are now warm and humid, but the sunbaked land they drift across is even warmer, and thus thunderstorms are likely to develop in the afternoon. If Tropical Gulf air manages to reach the western Great Plains and climb into the Rocky Mountains, sudden cloudbursts are possible. Moist Tropical Atlantic air can bring thunderstorms to the hot, green landscape of a New England summer, but if the same air arrives off the New England coast instead of spreading over the land, the cooler ocean waters can cause the formation of dense fog banks, as any Down-Easter can inform you.

West of the Rockies, the weather is governed by two moist, oceanic air masses—Tropical Maritime and Polar Maritime. Tropical Maritime air stays out over the ocean during spring, summer, and early fall, the clockwise winds at its edges providing the California coast with a steady flow of moist air out of the northwest. But when this marine air mass makes one of its winter visits to the mainland, the somewhat colder ground chills it, with rain the result. Tropical Maritime from the Pacific seldom moves farther east than the Rockies. Unlike Tropical Maritime air, Polar Maritime is likely to come ashore at any time of year. Since it is moist, it usually causes rain or snow as it moves eastward over the land, but by the time this cool, moist air reaches the Atlantic coast, as it may do in spring or fall, it has usually become dry and mild.

Among the anticyclones that influence the weather of Europe are the Polar Maritime from the Atlantic, Polar Continental from Siberia, and Tropical Continental from North Africa. Polar Maritime air is much like Polar Maritime from the Pacific; born in the North Atlantic Ocean, this maritime air has a moderating influence, can come ashore at any time of year, and frequently brings rain. In Europe, Polar

Although most western pines need the moist soil found on the western slopes of mountains, ponderosa pines, like these in Coconino National Forest, Arizona, are more drought-resistant and thrive on eastern slopes, where rain falls only infrequently.

Continental air is very much like Polar Continental from Canada, since it too is born in the dry interior of a continent. But when this cold air moves from Scandinavia to Britain in winter, it picks up moisture from the North Sea and becomes cloudy and damp; the English call this weather a "Black Northeaster." Sometimes this air works its way as far as southern Europe. When this happens it usually meets Tropical Continental air carried across the Mediterranean by a cyclone from Africa. This confrontation between two different kinds of air over the moist sea produces heavy showers, just as the meeting of dry Polar Continental and moist Tropical Gulf air does in the southern United States.

Not all of these great atmospheric domes are migratory throughout the year. Some are stationary during the winter, others during the summer, and a few are always found at the same place over the surface of the earth. The Polar Continental high tends to be stationary during the winter, although it often releases waves of piercingly cold weather into New England or the northern Great Plains. The Tropical Maritime

Cloudless skies and crystal-clear air are characteristic of the weather during the passage of a
high-pressure system.

high that lies off the coast of California is usually stationary during the warmer months, and is referred to as the Pacific High. Winds moving clockwise around the Pacific High guide storms along their course, just as in the late summer and fall the flow around the well-known Bermuda High in the tropical Atlantic steers hurricanes toward the Caribbean and even to the coast of the United States. In Eurasia, the polar air mass in Russia seldom visits Europe during the summer, and is often called the Siberian High. All of these stationary highs keep clear skies over the land or the ocean waters that spawned them, and all of them have attendant winds, moving clockwise, which control the movement of nearby storms and help to set up storm tracks.

These air masses and the distinctive air they contain can be compared to wines. Just as a connoisseur can tell you a wine's region, vineyard, and vintage from a single taste, so a fancier of air masses can step out on a sunny morning, draw a deep breath, and detect the special qualities of the air around him. "Polar Continental," he may announce, noting coolness, dryness, and a crisp and sparkling clarity, perhaps a scattering of small, puffy clouds high overhead, and even a hint of spruce or fir—all features of this special air from Canada. On the West Coast, he might say "Tropical Pacific": The air moist and warm, and, depending on the time of year, the sky either virtually free of clouds but hazy, or overcast and showery. At any time of year, there may be a tang of salt in the air from far out on the Pacific Ocean. In England, our expert will probably identify the Polar Maritime—cool, moist, and often bringing rain from the sea.

Air masses play a major role in determining weather everywhere in the world. The weather inside a stationary anticyclone is usually constant and generally clear—moist over the ocean and dry over the land. In a high-pressure system that is on the move, the weather is likely to be unstable—subject to change as the flowing air travels up over mountains, spills down the valleys, rushes forward in gusts and gales, slows down or stalls altogether, changes temperature, picks up moisture from lakes, rivers, and the sea, or sheds moisture as rain, snow, sleet, or hail. When two air masses meet or collide, as they often do, a weather front is formed; along such a front, almost anything is possible.

A Polar Continental air mass, like any other, can follow many routes and produce many sorts of weather. But except for occasional journeys to the Gulf of Mexico or California, the path of a Polar Continental air mass sooner or later leads to the Atlantic Ocean. When it leaves the land and heads out to sea, it again picks up moisture, and before long, the air mass and its distinctive features are lost in the swirl of westerly air currents that continually circle the globe, undisturbed by land forms in these temperate latitudes. Some of the air may be drawn into the Polar Atlantic air mass. But even as this Polar Continental air is dissolving in the general circulation over the sea or joining another air mass, an endless cycle is repeating itself. Thousands of miles away, in western Canada, more Polar Pacific air is flowing ashore, spilling down the eastern slopes of the Rockies, and setting the stage for the birth of a new Polar Continental air mass.

Treeless slopes are typical of the drier parts of the great interior lowland of Canada (OPPOSITE), the birthplace of air masses that bring clear weather to eastern North America.

(PAGES 58–59): After a winter storm front has crossed the mountains in western Wyoming, the snow gleams under the bright sunlight of another high-pressure system.

CHAPTER 3
THE LEADING EDGE: COLD FRONTS AND WARM FRONTS

LIKE A VICTORIOUS ARMY ADVANCING ACROSS THE FIELD against an enemy in retreat, the edge of a large air mass steadily pushes the air ahead of it. The very word *front*, used to refer to this mobile boundary between two air masses, was borrowed from the military language of World War I, less than two years after its end. Just as in a battle between two armies, most of the action in weather systems takes place along the front, often on a sharply defined line, where the two different air masses meet.

Fronts are either cold or warm, and the weather changes we experience depend on which of these fronts is passing over. As they approach, warm air is lifted aloft and expands, thereby reducing air pressure at ground level. A falling barometer is a good indication that a front is approaching.

But most fronts can be recognized by features more obvious than a falling barometer. Clouds gather, winds tend to pick up, rain or snow often falls, and for those who are outdoors to experience it, there is usu-

ally a marked change in temperature and wind direction when the front itself, the thin boundary dividing the old air mass from the newly arriving one, passes by. Both cold and warm fronts have these characteristics, but are very different in the types of clouds that accompany them, in the speed with which they travel, and in the time it takes the weather associated with them to pass.

Cold fronts travel faster and arrive more quickly than warm fronts. Because cold air is denser than warm air and therefore heavier, the leading edge of a cold front hugs the ground, plowing forward like a wedge and lifting the warm air ahead of it. Warm air meeting a cold front ascends; as it rises, it cools, the moisture it contains condensing into clouds. Such clouds form just ahead of the front, and are usually the first visible sign that a front is approaching. The first clouds we see are cumulus; these become larger and lower as the front nears. As the front itself arrives, a hard shower occurs. In summer, towering cumulo-

In this NASA satellite photograph, clouds marking the location of a front can be seen over the Mediterranean, where hot, dry continental air from the Sahara meets colder and moister air from Europe. Frontal activity can also be seen over South Africa, where Tropical Maritime and Polar Maritime air masses meet.

nimbus develop and thunderstorms with lightning and heavy rain can occur.

The retreating warm air is part of an air mass, too. If a cold air mass is coming from the northwest, as it usually is in the north temperate zone, air moving clockwise around the edge of the departing warmer air mass will flow from the southwest, parallel to the line of the advancing front. As the front itself approaches, accompanied by its showers, the temperature drops, and the wind shifts abruptly to the northwest, reflecting the forward movement of the new air mass. These sudden changes in temperature and wind direction are indications that the front has passed and the cold air mass itself has arrived. Barometric pressure stops falling and rises again as the deeper air of the new air mass flows overhead. The line of thick clouds moves by, and as the flow of cool, dry air continues, the skies clear, with only a few cumulus clouds drifting past. The cold front, and its attendant weather, traveling at a speed of 25 miles

In open country or at sea—where wide views of the sky are available—the arrival of a front can sometimes be seen clearly.

an hour or more, has passed within the space of a few hours.

A warm front moves more slowly, and the weather associated with it is usually gentler and longer lasting. As warm air invades a region, it rises above the denser cold air in front of it. Many miles ahead of the front itself, moist air, often tropical in origin, is gradually riding up over the cold air at the ground. As much as a few hundred miles away from an advancing warm front, the air will still feel dry, and the sky overhead may be clear. Although one cannot see it, the air aloft is already quite moist.

Eventually, delicate cirrus clouds, or "mare's tails," shaped by the polar jet stream miles above the earth, condense in the colder air. Formed at very high elevations, six to ten miles or more above the ground, cirrus are made of ice crystals, unlike most clouds, which are composed of water droplets. The vapor trails of jetliners, which normally dissipate quickly in dry air,

The gradual lowering and thickening of these clouds over the coast of southern Florida signals the arrival of a warm front.

(PAGES 64–65): High above Alaska's vast wilderness, the air is cold enough to freeze tiny droplets of water into delicate ice crystals—cirrus clouds that stream out ahead of an approaching front.

now last for longer periods, unable to evaporate in the moist air. Sometimes the sky becomes crisscrossed by the long, white streamers from aircraft. At this stage, the warm front, which may be traveling at a speed of only 15 miles an hour, may still be as much as one thousand miles—and up to three days—away.

Cirrus clouds and vapor trails do not always signal the arrival of a warm front; only when conditions advance to the next stage can we begin to be sure of an impending weather change. If a warm front is indeed on its way, the cirrus clouds will gradually grow denser, and start to appear at lower elevations. The delicate cirrus are eventually replaced by a thin, fairly uniform layer of altostratus clouds. At these middle elevations, clouds may be made up of either water droplets or ice crystals. The sky will now be overcast, with some texture in the clouds, but the sun can still be seen; sometimes a halo forms around the sun or the moon. The cloud cover grows ever thicker and lower and soon the sky is darkly overcast with a

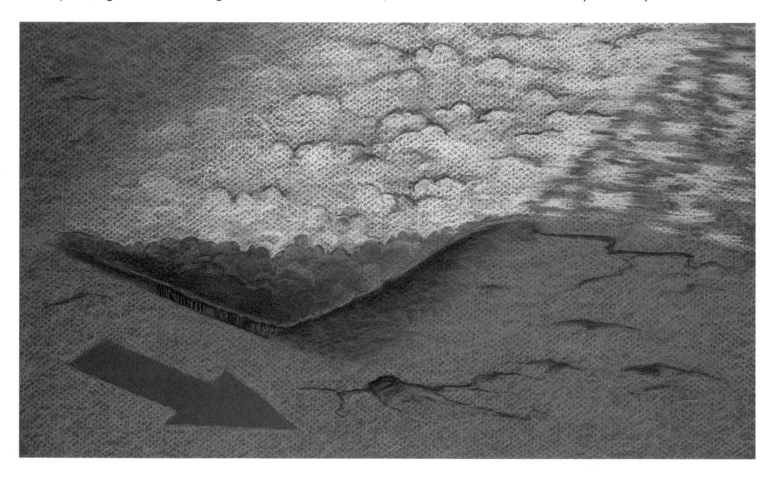

Preceded by high cirrus clouds, a warm front (seen here in cross-section) moves from left to right,
bringing a long period of steady rain.

featureless layer of nimbostratus cloud through which the sun is invisible; light but steady rain or snow then begins to fall.

Such a gentle, soaking rain may last for hours. Finally, the warm front itself arrives, accompanied by winds that swing from the south to the southwest or west. Since the cloud cover remains the same, and the rain or snow continues to fall, it is this shift in the direction of the wind, along with a rising barometer, that indicates the front has passed. The wind blew out of the south as long as the colder air mass was retreating northward, but the southwesterly or westerly winds are those that are flowing clockwise along the leading edge of the newly arrived warmer air mass. With the passage of the front, warmer air arrives. The precipitation continues for hours, even for a day or more, but eventually the cloud cover brightens and breaks, and we are in the midst of the new air mass.

Cold fronts and warm fronts are those experienced most often in North America and Eurasia. Similar

Traveling fast and ending abruptly, heavy rain accompanies a cold front (seen in cross-section), as it moves from left to right.

fronts occur in the southern hemisphere, where the flow of air around air masses is counterclockwise, producing a mirror image of what happens in the northern hemisphere. (Cold fronts move northward or flow onshore when cold maritime air moves in off the ocean; warm fronts travel southward.) Since there is much less land in temperate latitudes in the southern hemisphere than in the north, the oceans exert a moderating influence on the weather. Within a few degrees of the Equator, rising air creates a zone of relative calm, where fronts are few.

In fronts in the northern hemisphere, two important variations can occur. Sometimes an advancing front takes up a position parallel to the course of the polar jet stream. When this happens, the jet stream can no longer help push the front forward, and so the front slows and finally comes to a halt. A front can also stall if it meets a mountain range and is unable to cross over it. Such a stalled front is known as a stationary front. If it is oriented east to west, warm air from the south will ride up over the colder, northern air, and the clouds formed will produce steady rain or snow until the front either dissipates or succeeds in crossing the mountains, or the jet stream changes its position.

Another variation is known as an occluded front. Since warm fronts travel more slowly than cold fronts, a fast-moving cold front sometimes overtakes a warm front, lifting the warm air from the ground; rain or snow may then fall for days as a result. An occluded front can be associated with a frontal cyclone. High above the level of fronts moves the polar jet stream. As it flows eastward in the middle latitudes, a trough may appear along its course. Such troughs, where the atmosphere is shallow, alternate with ridges in which the atmosphere is deeper. At ground level beneath a trough the air pressure drops, while beneath a ridge the atmospheric pressure rises. These changes in pressure influence the circulation of air beneath them. Where the pressure is falling, a counterclockwise vortex of flowing air develops, producing a cyclone, or low-pressure system. If such a trough and its vortex lie above a front, they can cause one part of the front to move more rapidly southward as a cold front, while a section just to the east of the vortex is forced northward as a warm front. It is in the late stages of one of these frontal cyclones that the advancing cold front may overspread the air behind the warm front, lifting it off the ground and creating an occluded front.

Air circulating around the center of a cyclone converges inward like water flowing down a drain. But unlike such spiraling water, the incoming air cannot circle inward indefinitely. Crowded by pressure from the sides of the vortex, the air has nowhere to go except upward, and so it begins to rise. If the air rises high enough and is cooled sufficiently, its water vapor condenses into clouds; rain or snow may begin to fall. But in an air mass, the air is spiraling outward and is not forced to rise. The air is not crowded but is free to expand; as it expands and flows outward toward the edges of the air mass, it descends toward the ground and is warmed. As it grows warmer, its capacity to hold water vapor increases. The water vapor cannot condense into clouds, making clear skies and an absence of precipitation characteristic of the weather associated with air masses.

Frontal cyclones are also called depressions, low-

A fast-moving wall of dark, turbulent clouds accompanies the leading edge of a cold front.

pressure systems, or lows. By any name they are unlike any other feature of our weather. Once formed, they are free to move independently of the pattern of fronts, and generally travel eastward with the troughs that produced them, following the flow of the polar jet stream. In North America, frontal cyclones often develop in the lee of the Rocky Mountains. In Eurasia, they tend to form on the leeward side of mountain ranges in China. As they work their way eastward, these lows can develop into powerful storm systems,

spawning thunderstorms, smaller cyclones, and even tornadoes. Some of the largest have a diameter of as much as 1,000 miles.

As a cyclone moves from west to east, it very often carries along with it a trough of low pressure in the atmosphere that trails to the south of the center of the major low-pressure center. Smaller waves of low pressure formed by local conditions travel northward along this trough line. When such a trough reaches the Atlantic Ocean in eastern North America, or the Pa-

These low clouds are about to give way to heavy rain, and probably thunder and lightning, as the
thin leading edge of a cold front passes over a country road in Minnesota.

cific Ocean in eastern Asia, it may stall, and a succession of these smaller, secondary lows can move northeast one after another along the trough. Days may pass before the trough finally passes out to sea and dissolves, and clear weather returns.

Frontal cyclones are found in the middle latitudes, where the polar jet stream flows around the earth. Another kind of cyclone originates in the tropics, formed by disturbances along the line where the trade winds meet, between 10 degrees and 30 degrees North latitude and 10 degrees and 30 degrees South latitude, where the subtropical jet streams course eastward on either side of the Equator. A tropical cyclone begins as a small vortex, just as its temperate-zone counterpart does. Under the right conditions it can develop into a storm more mighty than any other on earth. Such storms have different names in different parts of the world. In the Indian Ocean, they are called tropical cyclones, but they are most widely known as typhoons or hurricanes.

Behind a front that has just crossed the rocky coast of Washington's Olympic Peninsula, a new air mass has arrived. The sky is clear again, glowing in the light of the setting sun.

(PAGES 72–73): In any year, the region around Tucson, Arizona, receives more than 30 thunderstorms, but seldom does one produce such a spectacular display of lightning as this.

CHAPTER 4

THE MARBLED SKY: CLOUDS

OURS HAS JUSTLY BEEN CALLED THE WATERY PLANET. Spreading away from the shore in all directions as oceans and seas, scattered across the land as lakes and ponds, flowing in rivers and streams, and covering high mountains and the polar regions with glaciers and ice caps, is water. Nearly 328,000 cubic miles of this unique, life-giving substance, weighing roughly 15 quintillion tons, cover more than 70 percent of the earth's surface and give it the brilliant blue color seen from outer space.

The atmosphere also contains water—billions of tons of it. As sunlight beats down on the earth, some of the water at the surface absorbs the sun's energy and evaporates into the air as separate molecules of water—invisible water vapor. There is always some water vapor present in the air. Even in the very driest deserts, where the air is clearest, water vapor still makes up about one tenth of one percent of the atmo-

sphere. As long as temperatures are high or the water vapor remains a gas, it is invisible; most people are not even aware of it. But as the water vapor ascends, it is cooled, which slows down the molecules of water. They adhere to microscopic particles of dust and form tiny droplets. Clusters of droplets form, and if a cluster is large enough, it finally becomes visible as a cloud.

Even in the clearest weather, the sun's radiation creates updrafts of warm air, or thermals, rising into the sky, and at the top of one of these columns, the water vapor in it condenses into a billowy white cloud with a rounded top and a flattened base, often shaped like a cauliflower. This is the cumulus cloud, a term coined, like all cloud names, from the Latin; *cumulus* means a pile or heap. By late morning on a warm, fair day, one can often see little fleets of these piles drifting over the landscape, their shadows following along beneath them on the ground.

(OPPOSITE): **Light cumulus, "fair-weather," clouds** (TOP), **formed by warm, moist air rising over Kauai in the Hawaiian islands drift downwind. During the passage of a high-pressure system, a fleet of newly formed cumulus clouds** (BOTTOM) **floats above a Midwestern field of goldenrod.**

(PAGES 76–77): **Dense cumulus congestus clouds have formed as moist air is pushed by the wind over the Antelope Mountains in Nevada.**

(PAGES 78–79): **By midday, these cumulus clouds have grown large and are combining. One of them may soon turn into a towering cumulonimbus.**

As the hours pass, these cumulus clouds may continue to grow. By afternoon, a growing cumulus cloud may have swelled into a great, dense mass, with majestic peaks and plunging valleys, the kind of cloud that is dark on the bottom and forms a gleaming landscape of its own when seen from the window of a passing airplane. Such a well-developed cumulus cloud, formed as more and more water condenses into droplets, is aptly called a cumulus congestus, from the word for "brought together." A cumulus congestus may tower as high as 20,000 feet—much higher than some of the billowy little clouds that formed earlier in the day. It often survives nighttime cooling, when thermals weaken and disappear.

Cumulus and cumulus congestus clouds owe their existence entirely to thermals. Sometimes the sun beats down fiercely on the ground, causing the air to heat more rapidly and rise more swiftly into the sky. Cumulus clouds loom ever larger, and tower ever higher. The lower surface of one of these growing cumulus clouds may still be only 3,000 feet from the ground, but its top now burgeons up as high as seven miles, into the region of the jet stream at 30,000 to 40,000 feet. Here winds shear off the top of the cloud, giving it an anvil shape. Delicate wisps of ice crystals, known as false cirrus, may trail away downwind.

But, serene as it may seem to the observer, the cloud is no longer a peaceful collection of water droplets, but a turbulent system of currents, powerful updrafts, and eddies. Collisions between water droplets or ice crystals cause the cloud to become charged with electricity. Positive charges accumulate at the top, and negative ones at the bottom. The rapidly rising air in one of these giants rises and expands, causing it to cool even more.

The once docile cumulus cloud has now become a violent and dangerous thundercloud, or cumulonimbus, a name coined from *nimbus*, a rainstorm. Forked lightning begins to dart out from the base of the cloud to the ground. Claps of thunder follow each bolt of lightning. Especially in desert regions where the bottom of a cumulonimbus is often higher above the ground than in more humid climates, a bolt of lightning may not strike directly beneath the cloud, but instead reach out for several miles before suddenly hitting the ground. Far from the storm itself, the sky might be clear, and one of these shafts of lightning, appearing without warning with no storm in sight, is quite literally a bolt from the blue. Heavy rain pours from the base of the cloud. As the thunderstorm reaches maturity, the updrafts within it are replaced by downdrafts, which cut off the supply of heat and moisture that has fed the rain produced by the cloud, and soon the storm weakens. The thunder becomes irregular and dies away, the lightning decreases in intensity, and the heavy rain is replaced by light showers. Eventually, the cumulonimbus, having exhausted itself, drifts away to be broken up by the wind.

Cumulonimbus clouds most often form in late afternoon after thermals have been rising. They also occur along advancing cold fronts, as warm, moist air is forced aloft. Sometimes they form in mountains, when wind forces moist air to high elevations. If the wind blowing up the slope of a mountain is strong, it will reach the top and then, instead of sliding down the leeward slope, it will continue to rise, so that the cloud forms over the peak. Under these conditions, the result is a growing cumulus, which can eventually reach a size where it becomes a cumulonimbus. Thunder then begins to rumble among the mountains.

Although lightning is dangerous, most thunderstorms do little real damage. But an unusually severe one can cause destructive winds or hailstorms, and in deserts a cloudburst can cause flooding. The more severe a thunderstorm is, the more likely it is to be accompanied by tornadoes.

Cumulus, cumulus congestus, and cumulonimbus clouds are all classified as vertical clouds because they form from vertically rising thermals, and can occur at almost any elevation. Other major cloud types are found only at certain elevations and are therefore classified by altitude as high clouds, middle clouds, or low clouds.

The top of a large cumulonimbus may reach a height of 12 miles, but the so-called high clouds usually range only about six or seven miles above the ground, and may be as low as four miles in polar regions. At these frigid levels, they contain ice crystals. The most distinctive of the high clouds is the cirrus cloud, which is characterized by its wispy or fibrous shape, well expressed by its name, which is Latin for a curl of hair. (They are also known as mare's tails.) Cirrus clouds are formed by high-level winds that draw the cloud out into delicate streamers, so thin that they are always white. At their downwind ends they are often curled upward. These clouds can be the first sign that a storm or warm front is approaching, but all one can say for sure is that they reveal the presence of moisture at these great heights. Although cirrus are driven by strong winds, their high altitude causes them to seem almost motionless against the clear blue of the sky. With their light, fleecy shape, they are among the most beautiful of all the clouds.

Another of the high clouds is cirrocumulus, which consists of a high, thin layer of white ice crystals that is broken into regular bands or rows of more or less distinct small tufts, which look like tiny cumulus clouds, by rising currents of air that have interfered with the horizontal winds that would otherwise have produced cirrus clouds. Like cirrus, a sheet of cirrocumulus can be a sign that a storm is on the way, but all that is certain is that the air is unstable,

Seen at a distance over the flat country of southern Arizona, this cumulonimbus has assumed the anvil shape of a typical thunderhead; somewhere beneath it rain is falling.

(PAGES 82–83): With a few high cirrus clouds ahead of it, a thunderstorm arrives at Crescent Lake in the White Mountains of Arizona.

While this thundercloud has not risen high enough for the jet stream to give its top the shape of an anvil, it has already begun to shed rain, and has even formed a rainbow.

(OPPOSITE): Night is coming and Tucson has already turned its lights on, but the top of this cumulonimbus cloud is high enough for the sun still to shine on it.

and that rising air currents have broken the thin layer into these small, regular parcels.

If a warm front really is approaching, cirrus or cirrocumulus clouds eventually give way to a sheet of cirrostratus. Cirrostratus (*stratus* means spread out) is a milky, translucent layer of ice crystals that develops at the same altitude as a cirrus cloud if the amount of moisture increases. Cirrostratus may be white or pale gray, and is translucent, so that the sun and moon can be seen through it. Halos often appear around the sun or moon when viewed through a layer of cirrostratus. As a storm or front grows nearer, the layer of cirrostratus thickens.

The middle clouds are found at altitudes of 15,000 to 20,000 feet, and are made up either of ice crystals or water droplets. As a storm approaches, a layer of cirrostratus lowers, thickens, and grades into a gray and featureless layer known as altostratus. Unlike cirrostratus, altostratus (from *altus*, high) is usually so thick that it obscures the sun. Altostratus may produce rain or snow, but often this cloud type is sufficiently high that precipitation evaporates before it reaches the ground. If it thickens and lowers, however, altostratus may change into a dense nimbostratus, one of the low clouds.

Altocumulus clouds resemble a sheet, or layer, of cirrocumulus, but these billowy cloudlets are both lower and larger, and typically lack the delicate appearance of high cirrocumulus. This cloud type is sometimes made up of water droplets rather than ice crystals. The cloudlets may be arranged in the same regular rows as those in a layer of cirrocumulus, but their greater depth makes their undersides darker, and so altocumulus has a more strongly textured appearance, and is never pure white. Although it is thicker than cirrocumulus, altocumulus still transmits sunlight. As in cirrocumulus, the patterned look of altocumulus clouds is evidence of unstable air aloft, but is not necessarily associated with an approaching storm or front.

Layers of altocumulus are quite variable, and with their larger and more irregular cloudlets, they can be difficult to distinguish from a wind-torn layer of stratus, or from the low-cloud type known as stratocumulus. But one type of altocumulus is fairly distinctive, and has been given a name of its

With the sun sinking behind the Matopo Hills in Zimbabwe, a layer of altocumulus clouds catches its peach-colored rays.

(OPPOSITE): As low-lying fog covers the northern end of San Francisco Bay (TOP), early morning reveals wisps of cirrus clouds high overhead. (BOTTOM) Over the Anza-Borrego Desert in southern California, a thin layer of cirrocumulus clouds takes on a delicate pink at sunrise.

Formed by wind in the freezing air high above the Sonoran Desert of southern Arizona, delicate bands of cirrus resemble ripple marks on a beach.

(OPPOSITE): A layer of cirrostratus (TOP) so thin that the sun can be seen clearly through it is usually a sign that rainy weather is on the way. At dusk, a layer of altostratus (BOTTOM) forms a pattern of small cloudlets and bands, similar to cirrocumulus but lower and thicker.

(PAGES 90–91): Usually formed of ice crystals, a layer of altostratus can be thin enough to be translucent, but still too thick to allow the sun to be seen through it.

own. When altocumulus forms, the heat released as the water vapor condenses may cause the air in the cloud layer to rise; small towers develop on some of the cloudlets. These make the cloudlets taller than those one sees in clusters of normal cumulus clouds. The turreted cloudlets resemble small hilltop fortresses, and so the name of this cloud type is altocumulus castellanus (from *castellanus*, of a fort). Altocumulus castellanus is especially beautiful at sunset, when its towers glow with pink or pale orange. Although this cloud type often appears in unstable air that is about to develop showers or even to produce cumulonimbus clouds, it does not shed rain itself.

Of the low clouds, stratus is the most familiar. Like cirrostratus and altostratus, simple stratus is a layer, but one that is thicker and grayer; it tends to hug the ground. This is the cloud of those dull, darkly overcast days when there may be drizzle or very fine snow; but real rain, though it always seems imminent, never arrives. Stratus often lies almost motionless over the

As currents of warm air rise above an approaching storm, towers develop on the tops of gathering altocumulus clouds, giving them the name cumulus castellanus.

land, less than a mile and a half up. It forms from condensation at low elevations and can resemble fog, but unlike fog it never rests on the ground. There is usually little wind associated with a layer of stratus, but sometimes light gusts play beneath it, giving its underside a ragged appearance. If the wind picks up a bit, the cloud may be partly torn into fragments; such wind-torn stratus is called fractostratus (from *fractus*, broken).

Although stratus commonly develops in humid air over flat country, it can also form in mountains. If a moisture-laden layer of air is forced over a mountain ridge by a gentle but persistent wind, it may reach an elevation at which the water vapor condenses into a layer that lies over the crest of the ridge. The air continues to flow down the mountain's leeward slope, but here the water droplets evaporate again and disappear. Although there is a continuous flow of air over the ridge, the layer of cloud is visible only on the ridge top, seemingly balanced over the highest

Above the pack ice north of Point Barrow, Alaska, a sheet of textured cirrocumulus grades into a featureless layer of cirrostratus.

ground. Such a layer of stratus, formed over a range of mountains, is called orographic stratus. Orographic stratus can be dangerous to mountain climbers because it reduces visibility and because in the cold air, snow or rain is more likely to fall than when a stratus layer overlies a coastal plain.

Another of the low clouds is stratocumulus. As its name implies, it has some of the features of both stratus and cumulus clouds. Stratocumulus forms when a low-lying sheet of stratus breaks into lumpy, gray and white masses with blue sky showing between them. It can also form in just the opposite way, when cumulus clouds join into a broken layer. Not surprisingly, every gradation between an almost featureless layer of stratus and a widespread fleet of cumulus clouds is possible, and identification of stratocumulus can sometimes be difficult. Adding to the confusion is the resemblance between altocumulus and stratocumulus. Stratocumulus is closer to the ground, always less than a mile and a half up. Its

This steadily thickening layer of stratus clouds at Port Clyde on the coast of Maine means that a warm front is approaching, bringing rainy weather.

pattern of white and gray patches is larger, and often more irregular, than that of altocumulus.

The largest of the low clouds, and the only one that can be depended upon to produce rain or snow, is the nimbostratus (storm-layer) cloud. It ranges from less than a mile to about four miles above the ground, and is a very thick, dark gray, uniform layer of cloud. It is usually among the clouds that approach with a low-pressure system, and often forms from a strato-cumulus cloud that has thickened and lowered. Al-though we cannot see it, a nimbostratus cloud may have a layer of altostratus lying directly above it. Very often, ragged, wind-blown shreds of cloud called "scud" slide along beneath a nimbostratus, but some-times the bottom of one of these large rain-bearers is concealed by a layer of true stratus. A passing nim-bostratus may come near enough to the ground to conceal the tops of tall buildings or low hills. Like a cumulonimbus, nimbostratus produces rain or snow, but because it moves more slowly and is constantly

A thick layer of stratus clouds lies over San Francisco, but afternoon sunlight manages to flood in beneath it, indicating that clear weather is on the way.

renewed as its parent storm system approaches, it can shed rain for hours, rather than producing the brief but violent downpour we expect from a cumulonimbus before it has dissipated. In winter, very deep snowfalls can occur before a nimbostratus has finally moved through an area.

Although the clouds discussed so far are the most common and distinctive kinds, other cloud types, formed under more unusual circumstances, are also recognized by meteorologists. One of the most unusual in appearance is the lenticular cloud. A stratus cloud may form above a mountain ridge as moist air moves up a slope, over the top, and down the other side. Sometimes the current of moist air behaves like the water in a stream that flows over a submerged boulder. What is evident to the eye is a raised spot in the stream over the hidden rock, followed by several undulations downstream as the current repeatedly rises and falls in a series of "echoes" of the original wave. The water continues to flow, but the waves stay in the same place. In a current of air that behaves like this, the water vapor repeatedly moves in and out of the higher zone where the temperature is cold enough to cause condensation, and we see a long series of lens-shaped clouds extending away from the mountain peak where the undulations began. These clouds are called lenticular and, while not common, are among the most striking of all.

Another unusual cloud develops from cumulus that move into an area of high turbulence. Known as mammatocumulus (from *mammatus*, with breasts), they are stratocumulus clouds that have small protuberances on their undersides, instead of the flattened bases typical of cumulus. Mammatocumulus clouds usually form in association with eddies of air in the violent turbulence that precedes severe thunderstorms.

Because they need a terminology that is as specific as possible, meteorologists have coined many more names for variations in the common cloud types. If a layer of altocumulus is very thin, for example, and transmits much of the sun's light, it may be termed an altocumulus translucidus. If a sheet of cirrocumulus develops a series of waves produced by the wind, it is called a cirrocumulus undulatus.

While all of these names are Latin, or derived from Latin, none was used by the Romans. In Rome, all clouds were referred to by the word *nube*, which is related to the word *nebula*, or mist. Our modern Latin names for clouds were first used in the early 1800s by Luke Howard, a London pharmacist who was trying to classify the various shapes of clouds he saw. The names are purely descriptive and came into use long before the dynamics of clouds were understood. But the names were necessary to that understanding because they made it possible to distinguish between cloud types.

Mammatocumulus (OPPOSITE) is usually found in the vicinity of violent thunderstorm activity and is often a harbinger of tornadoes. Lenticular clouds (PAGES 98 AND 99, BOTTOM) are seldom seen. They are motionless, but the moisture in them is moving, first into a layer of cold air where it condenses, then back down into a warmer layer where it evaporates. A spectacular "wave" cloud (PAGE 98, TOP) was formed in this same manner.

(PAGE 99, TOP): A layer of orographic stratus above Mount Lassen in northern California. (PAGES 100–101): Altocumulus is easily distinguished from cirrocumulus by its pattern of white, sunlit clouds and gray shadows.

CHAPTER 5

HEAT WAVES AND COLD SNAPS: TEMPERATURE AND ITS EFFECTS

FROM THE CENTER OF THE SOLAR SYSTEM THE SUN RADIATES A colossal amount of energy outward in all directions. Only one two-billionth of this solar energy reaches our small planet after its eight-minute journey of 93 million miles, but the quantity is still enormous: some 180,000 trillion watts every second. This energy not only includes heat, but various forms of electromagnetic radiation, mainly ultraviolet and infrared rays and visible light. Of the huge amount of heat that reaches the earth, about 42 percent is reflected directly back into space, another 15 percent is absorbed by the earth's atmosphere, and the remaining 43 percent actually penetrates to the earth's surface, where it is either absorbed or reflected back into the atmosphere.

By absorbing heat, our blanket of atmospheric gases keeps temperatures near the ground within the range in which water occurs as liquid, water vapor, and ice, and in which life can exist. The atmosphere also protects the earth and its living things from the extreme heat of solar radiation. In the higher reaches of the atmosphere, about 50 miles up, gases are so thin that measurements of temperature, which are really measurements of the energy level of molecules, become meaningless; there are so few molecules of any kind at these great altitudes that a thermometer is useless. With no gases at these heights to absorb the sun's energy, all objects—including thermometers, satellites, and the protective outer garments worn by astronauts—are exposed to the full power of radiation from the sun.

Our atmosphere also dampens the pronounced temperature changes that would otherwise occur each day as the earth revolves, causing areas of its surface to sink into shadow. The importance of this moderating effect can be realized by considering the lifeless surface of the moon, where there is no atmosphere at all. At midday on the sunlit side of the moon,

Where water covers the floor of the desert and is then dried by the extreme heat, the result is often
a pattern of cracked mud so orderly it almost looks manmade.

(PAGES 104–105): Ground fog rises and begins to dissipate as the early morning air of spring
becomes warmer. (PAGES 106–107): A warm mist drifts through the tropical cloud forest at
Monteverde National Park in Costa Rica.

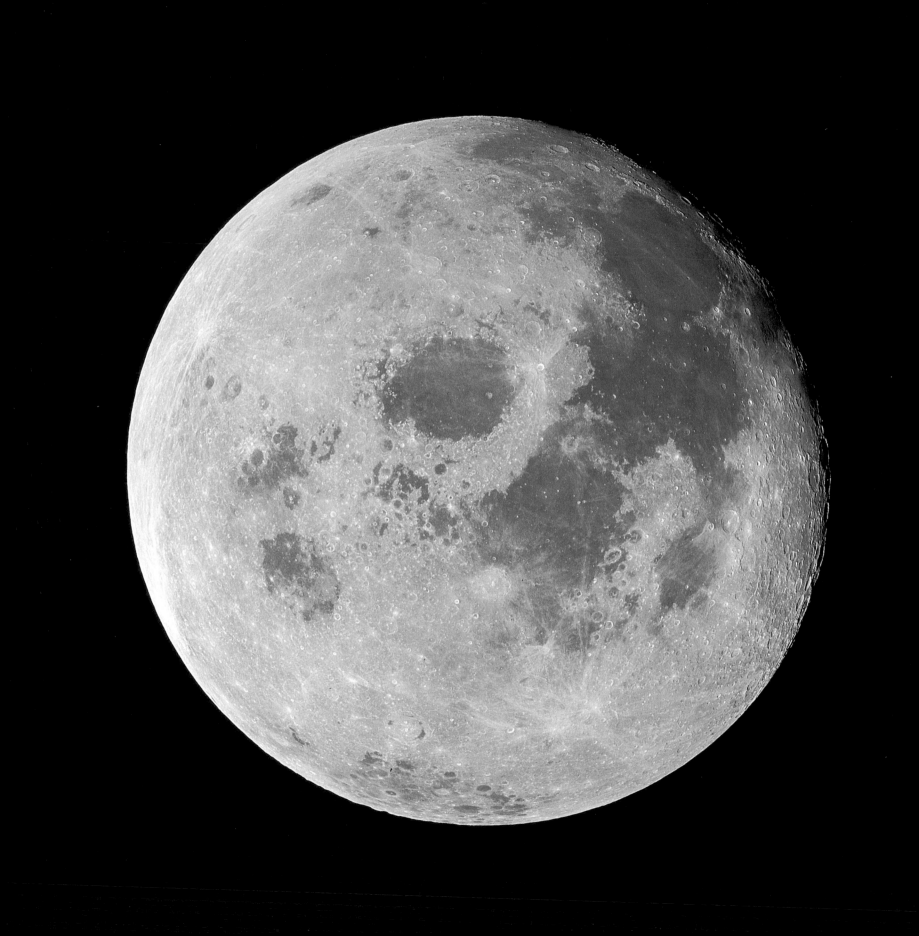

the temperature is about 261°F (127°C). On the dark side of the moon, where the surface is sheltered from solar radiation, the temperature drops to −243°F (−153°C), a daily fluctuation of more than 500°F (280°C).

The greatest amounts of heat and light reach the earth's equatorial regions, where the sun is most often directly overhead. Much less heat reaches the poles, where the sun's rays arrive on a slant, which requires them to pass through more of the earth's atmosphere. During the summer in either hemisphere, when the pole is tilted toward the sun, more heat and light reach the high latitudes; the other hemisphere, which is then receiving solar radiation on a slant, experiences colder temperatures. Any area exposed to the sun, unprotected by a layer of clouds that reflects heat back into the upper atmosphere or into space, heats more rapidly, and to higher temperatures, than areas around it. Even the surface of a parking lot heats up more quickly than neighboring shady lawns or woodlands. The result of these and other inequalities, both global and local, is that heat is not distributed evenly over the earth.

When the molecules of the heated atmosphere take up the sun's energy, they begin to move faster. This causes atmospheric gases to expand and become less dense, and because air that is less dense than the air surrounding it also weighs less, the heated air begins to rise. Air that has been heated at the Equator rises and begins to flow toward the poles. At the earth's surface, colder, heavier air flows toward the Equator to replace the air that is warming and ascending into the atmosphere. Any area whose surface is warmer than those surfaces around it sends aloft an updraft of heated air, and cooler, neighboring air slides in to replace it. An intricate pattern of circulation—rising warm air and descending colder air—acts to redistribute heat both in the atmosphere and at ground level. This redistribution of heat in the earth's atmosphere is a never-ending process, one that is responsible for much of our weather. But it never manages to even out temperatures at the surface because solar radiation constantly heats some places more than others.

The hottest places on earth are not on the Equator, but in zones just to its north and south. In these twin bands on either side of the Equator, roughly in the zone of the horse latitudes, where skies are nearly always clear and the unobstructed rays of the sun strike the surface almost constantly, lie some of the world's great deserts—the Sahara and Kalahari in Africa, the Great Indian Desert in India and Pakistan, the Empty Quarter in Arabia, the Great Sandy Desert of Australia, and the Atacama Desert in Chile. It is in these places the world's hottest temperatures are found. The highest reading ever taken on earth was 136°F (58°C), recorded on September 13, 1922, in the shade

From our viewpoint, the moon may look cold, but its surface has no atmosphere to protect it from the sun's rays and it reaches a temperature of 261° Fahrenheit.

(PAGES 110–111): During the hot, rainless season in Botswana, as elsewhere in Africa, elephants perform a vital service for other animals by digging "wells" to reach water that has receded far below the surface of ponds and marshes.

at Al'Aziziyah, Libya, in the Sahara Desert, more than 30 degrees north of the Equator. The highest reading in North America was nearly as great, 134°F (57°C) at Death Valley, California, on July 10, 1913. The place with the highest annual average temperature, a staggering 94°F (35°C), is Dalul in the Danakil Desert of Ethiopia, about 15 degrees north of the Equator.

Just as the hottest places are not on the Equator, the coldest are not at the poles. The South Pole is located on a continent, where temperatures are not moderated by nearby oceans. The world's coldest spot is on Antarctica's high, icy plateau between the South Pole and the Indian Ocean; at Plateau Station, the annual average temperature is −70°F (−57°C). This plateau is also the site of the lowest temperature ever recorded: At the Soviet station of Vostok, about 800 miles from the South Pole, a temperature of −129°F (−89°C) was recorded on July 21, 1983. The North Pole lies not on a continent but over a frozen ocean, and the water beneath the ice is supercooled to 28°F (−2°C), but even the water's low temperature is enough to prevent the temperature in the vicinity of the pole from dropping to extreme levels. The coldest reading ever taken in the northern hemisphere was −90°F (−68°C); it occurred both at Verkhoyansk, Siberia, on February 5 and 7, 1933, and at Oimekon, Siberia, on February 6 of the same year. The lowest temperature in North America was −81°F (−63°C), recorded at Snag, in the Yukon, on February 3, 1947.

As air circulates about the globe, a layer of cold air sometimes comes to lie above a mass of warmer air in what is called an inversion. This can occur on clear nights when heat radiates upward from the ground; the cold ground chills the air just above it. The loss of heat from the surface begins soon after sundown and continues through the night if the sky remains clear. The air in an inversion is quite stable; little mixing takes place between the warm layer and the cooler layer above it. As a result, smoke from smokestacks and exhaust pipes cannot disperse, but instead spreads out as a layer of air pollution. The Los Angeles Basin, parts of Arizona, certain valleys in the Rocky Mountains, and the Thames Valley around London are places where inversions commonly occur. Most inversions dissipate the following day, as temperatures equalize, but sometimes an inversion persists for days. The accumulated air pollution, or smog, can reach levels that are dangerous to health. The worst inversion occurred in London in December 1952. Fog that had combined with sulphur compounds in coal smoke created a dense layer of smog that hugged the ground. People in theaters reported that they could not see the stage. Airplanes were forced to make instrument landings. Several people walked off docks into the Thames, and were almost impossible to locate and rescue. The sound of coughing and choking could be heard everywhere. When the air finally cleared after four days, 4,000 had died, and hospitals were filled with people suffering from bronchitis and asthma. Another inversion, the "Big Smog" of 1948 in the coal town of Donora, Pennsylvania, near Pittsburgh, caused 2,500 illnesses and 20 deaths.

Some locations on earth experience only slight changes in temperature. In the town of Garapan, on Saipan in the Northern Mariana Islands, the temperature was monitored between 1927 and 1935. Dur-

Although it is the southernmost point on the planet, the South Pole does not have the coldest temperatures; that distinction belongs to the high plateau that lies between the pole and the Indian Ocean.

Although it looks like the drifting snow of warmer climes, the wind-carved ice, or *sastrugi* (TOP), of
Antarctica is both beautiful and treacherous.

Spring in Antarctica. As the temperature rises, the sea ice at McMurdo Sound (BOTTOM) is cracked
into plates by the action of ocean currents and the wind.

Icebergs are always present around Antarctica (TOP), but in summer the slightly warmer water and
the action of waves carve the icebergs into fantastic shapes.

(BOTTOM): For much of the year in polar regions, the sea is frozen; outposts and research stations
are accessible by water only after the way has been cleared by icebreakers.

ing these nine years, the temperature varied from a high of 88°F (31°C), recorded on September 9, 1931, to a low of 67°F (19°C), recorded on January 30, 1934, a range of only 21°F (12°C). But most places have a greater range than that. Verkhoyansk in Siberia, where the lowest temperature in the northern hemisphere was recorded, has still another distinction. The warmest temperature ever recorded there was 98°F (36°C), while the coldest confirmed reading was −90°F (−68°C), a temperature range of 188°F (104°C), the greatest known anywhere on earth. The record for a change in a single 24-hour period belongs to the town of Browning, Montana, headquarters of the Blackfeet Indian Reservation. On January 23, 1916, the thermometer stood at a comfortable 44°F (6°C). During the night, a strong cold wave moved

In the chilly air, water vapor from a nuclear power plant forms tall plumes of steam (ABOVE).

Even in hot, dry Arizona, the nights can be cold and a mist from the Colorado River often steals into the Grand Canyon (OPPOSITE, TOP).

In some places, such as the power plant in Victorville, California (OPPOSITE, BOTTOM), the sun's energy is trapped before it can radiate back into the sky. The 960,000 cells on 108 tracking panels harness solar energy for human needs.

(PAGES 116–117): Smog held at ground level by a temperature inversion almost hides the domes and spires of the Taj Mahal at Agra, India.

down from the north. By dawn, the thermometer read −56°F (−49°C). In less than one day, the temperature had dropped 100°F (55°C), a rapid change that has never been matched anywhere else in the world.

Although dramatic temperature changes, and severe cold and heat in general, can pose health hazards, the human body has defenses that act to maintain its normal temperature of 98.6°F. Our physiological response to cold is shivering, in which mus-cles contract rapidly to generate heat, and blood vessels of the skin contract to reduce heat loss to the surrounding air. In high heat, perspiration increases and its evaporation cools the skin. In spite of the dramatic extremes and fluctuations in the earth's temperature, and the arrival and departure of cold snaps and heat waves, the thermometer generally stays within a range to which humans and all other animals as well as plants are adapted.

Although this bull elk (ABOVE) came down from the windswept highlands in the fall, it has not escaped harsh winter weather. It still must use its hooves to scrape away snow to find food.

Sometimes snow falls in the Sonora Desert of Arizona (OPPOSITE), transforming the cactus, ocotillo, and palo verde into striking gardens of white. Such snowfalls usually melt quickly and do these plants no harm.

CHAPTER 6
WHEN DRY LEAVES FLY: WIND AND WINDSTORMS

As THE EARTH SPINS ON ITS AXIS, ITS ROTATION AND THE heating of the atmosphere by the sun maintain a global system of flowing air, a giant pattern of winds. On either side of the Equator, where heated air is rising and beginning to move poleward, a zone of low pressure and high humidity called the doldrums extends around the globe. This sultry air may stir with variable breezes, but just as often it is undisturbed by wind for days, or even weeks, at a time. Here, "as idle as a painted ship upon a painted ocean," the barque of Coleridge's Ancient Mariner was becalmed in punishment for his killing of an albatross.

The misfortunes of the Ancient Mariner might never have occurred had he been a little farther to the north or south, at a latitude of about 30 degrees. Here the trade winds blow more or less constantly, out of the northeast in the northern hemisphere and from the southeast in the southern hemisphere. The trade winds represent some of the air that has ascended at the Equator and, after becoming cooler, has descended and is flowing back to replace air newly lifted by the sun's heat. His ship would have made good progress on these dependable breezes that cool many tropical islands and speed vessels on their way.

A short distance beyond, however, at about 30 to 35 degrees latitude, he would have found himself in another belt of calm, known as the horse latitudes. Here the air that feeds the trade winds is descending toward the earth's surface; the barometric pressure is high, and breezes, when they spring up, are light and variable. No one is sure how the horse latitudes got their name; some say they are named for the horses that died of thirst aboard ships stalled in this zone of calm, and had to be thrown overboard before reaching their destination in the West Indies.

When, as he eventually did, Coleridge's Mariner reached the region to the north of 35 degrees, he found himself in a zone of strong westerlies and quickly sailed back to England and told his sad tale. The prevailing westerlies, which lie between 35 and

In one of the most famous of all Dust Bowl images, a farmer and his sons race for shelter from the strafing of wind-blown topsoil in Cimarron County, Oklahoma.

A dune in White Sands National Monument, New Mexico (PAGES 124–125), releases a plume of sand into the wind. Although only a small amount of sand moves at any one time, over the centuries such wind-battered dunes can travel many miles.

about 60 degrees North latitude, and in the same zone in the southern hemisphere, are guided by the Coriolis force, which turns the winds to the east to form the polar jet streams as the earth spins to the west. Surface winds in the southern hemisphere are generally stronger and more persistent than those in the northern hemisphere because they are not interrupted by large land masses; here, they are known as the roaring forties.

In polar regions, beyond the prevailing westerlies, winds tend to flow eastward—clockwise in the north and counterclockwise in the south—because there is usually a high-pressure system over each of the poles. These polar anticyclones are called the arctic (or antarctic) semi-permanent highs. It was on the edge of the antarctic high that the Ancient Mariner encountered the fateful albatross.

These prevailing winds and calms form the general pattern of circulation of the earth's atmosphere. But this system is only "prevailing," not permanent. Modifying the general pattern are many local and seasonal winds. A number of these are found in

the zone of prevailing westerlies. One of the most famous of these is the *mistral*, a cold, blustery, alpine wind that is funneled down the valley of the Rhône and strikes the French Riviera with gusts as high as 90 miles an hour. Another mountain wind is the *bora*, whose name is derived from that of Boreas, the Greek god of the north wind. The *bora* is a harsh, cold, winter wind that blows down from the eastern Alps into Dalmatia and onto the east coast of Italy, accompanied by plunging temperatures, snow, and heavy seas on the Adriatic.

In North America, the most famous wind is the chinook, a sudden warm wind that is liable to sweep down the eastern slopes of the Rockies and onto the Great Plains. In winter, a chinook is usually welcomed for its warmth, which results from its rapid descent and lack of moisture. Winter chinooks are sometimes called "snow-eaters," and indeed, the change in temperature they produce can be dramatic. On the morning of January 22, 1943, a chinook arrived without warning at Spearfish, South Dakota, and the temperature rose from −4°F (−20°C) to 45°F (7°C) in an astonishing two minutes. A similar

When they can be seen, the effects of wind are rarely more beautiful than when they create plumes of snow on mountain peaks.

wind, called the *foehn*, is liable to descend out of the Alps at any season. It is so dry that crops look scorched in its wake, and smoking is prohibited in Swiss villages to lessen the risk of forest fires.

The monsoon winds of India are complex. During the winter, a strong, dry, northeast wind blows down from a high-pressure system in Siberia. In summer, another wind, this one laden with moisture from the Indian Ocean, blows back from the southwest, causing heavy rains in much of southern Asia. Both are called the monsoon because it was once thought that they were the same wind, which was blowing back and forth with the seasons.

Winds that are not born in alpine regions often owe their existence to an absence of mountains. On the Great Plains, there is no barrier between the Arctic and Texas. When a cold air mass rolls down out of Canada, unimpeded by anything taller than a fence post, its frigid wind is called a norther. In spring in the Mediterranean region, the hot, dusty wind of the Sahara is drawn to the coast by low-pressure systems. Called *leveche* in Morocco, *levante* in Spain, *khamsin* in Egypt, and *sharav* in Israel, this desert wind is known generally as the sirocco. At its worst, it Is called *simoom*, Arabic for "the poisoner." At such times this wind can carry violent dust storms as far as the northern part of southern Europe.

These local winds are dependable, if unpleasant, but much more unpleasant are certain cyclonic winds. Under the right circumstances, these more erratic winds can be the most destructive on earth. Chief among these is the hurricane.

Paradoxically, hurricanes are born in the doldrums, where there is often no wind at all. Warm, moist air at the earth's surface begins to rise and, as it does, cooler air moves in quickly at ground level to replace it. This cooler air spirals in cyclonically—counterclockwise in the northern hemisphere, clockwise south of the Equator. Only ocean water that is warmer than 80°F (27°C) can supply the energy necessary for such cloud spirals to form. Water that is this warm is most likely to be found north of the Equator between May and November, and south of the Equator during the other half of the year. In the northern hemisphere these cyclones are most common in

Modest compared to the giant dust storms of the American Midwest in the 1930s, this one in southern Morocco can still carry its fine particles as far as southern Europe.

September. At this early stage, such a cyclone is called a tropical disturbance, and at any one time, there are many tropical disturbances gently spinning in the region of the doldrums around the globe. Unlike cyclones in temperate regions, there is no front associated with the birth of one of these subtropical cyclones. Without a front nearby, temperatures, air pressure, cloud cover, and wind speeds remain symmetrical around the center of a tropical disturbance as it spins majestically over the water. A tropical disturbance appears on satellite photographs as a solid, roughly circular patch of clouds.

Most tropical disturbances don't "take," but simply dissolve back into the placid airflow patterns of the doldrums. But if it doesn't dissipate, a tropical disturbance begins to drift westward under the influence of the trade winds. Because it is moving over seas whose warmth supplies it with energy, it begins to grow. Its diameter, cloud cover, and wind speed increase, while the air pressure at its center decreases. When the barometric pressure at its center becomes so low that one or more isobars—lines on a weather map that link places with the same air pressure—are closed circles, the disturbance becomes a tropical depression. The wind speed of a tropical depression is still less than 38 miles an hour.

The growing tropical depression continues to creep westward or northward. When its wind speed surpasses 39 miles an hour, it is classified as a tropical storm. By now, meteorologists have already been watching it carefully for some time. Strong winds circle around this closed storm system; high walls of cloud build up around its center; and a distinctive spiral pattern shows up on satellite photographs.

Such a tropical storm may show an open spot—the eye—at its center. Because many tropical storms do some damage, most governments issue tropical-storm warnings. But the majority of these storms eventually weaken and disappear when they move northward over colder water or when they come ashore. A few continue to grow in size and wind speed, and when winds blowing around the center of one of these systems reach a speed of 75 miles an hour, the storm has "arrived." It is now a great vortex of dangerous winds, classified as a hurricane.

Since hurricanes develop from disturbances that form in warm equatorial waters and tend to drift westward, they occur most often in the western Atlantic, western Pacific, and the tropical parts of the Indian Ocean; a few form in the eastern Pacific, over warm waters off the coast of Mexico. The paths of these storms take them, respectively, toward the West Indies, where the word "hurricane" originated, into the China Sea, where they are called typhoons, to the Philippines, where a hurricane is known as a *baguio*, to Japan, where the word is *reppu*, or toward the shores of the Indian Ocean, where the general term cyclone has been used for them since 1856. In Australia, where hurricanes strike at the end of the southern-hemisphere summer, they are called "willy-willies." Under any name, a hurricane is a colossal and dangerous weather system, the most destructive storm on earth.

Having moved westward, most hurricanes in the northern hemisphere turn to the north as they leave the zone of the trade winds. Those spawned in the western Atlantic usually move into the Caribbean and cause damage in the Lesser Antilles, which are

(OPPOSITE): **Satellites not only help predict the path and speed of hurricanes, they have also provided important ways of understanding the physics of these monster storms. These NASA satellite views show hurricanes in various stages and from several vantage points and distances.**

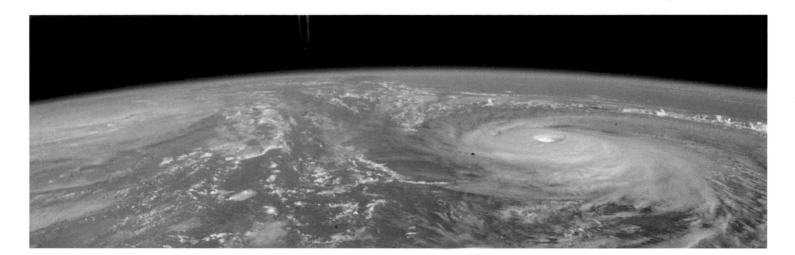

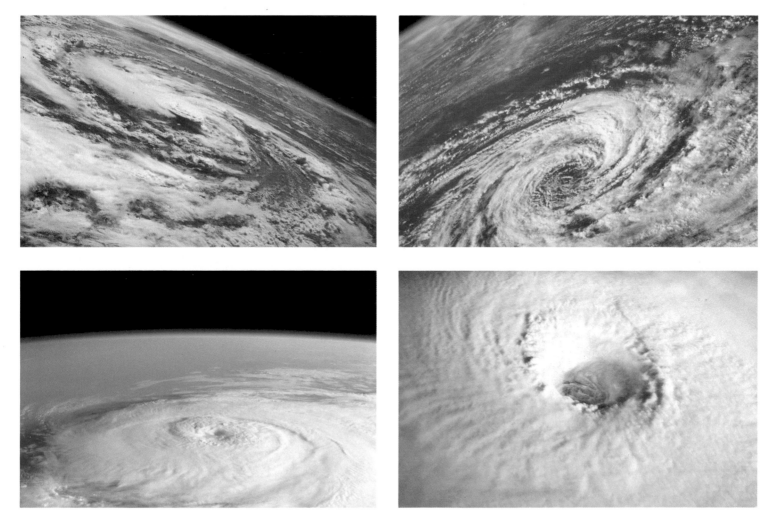

aligned north-to-south in a row that lies directly in the path of most of these huge storms. Their diameter can reach 300 miles; the eye of one of these hurricanes, where air pressure is lowest, can be more than 25 miles across. The wall of clouds surrounding the eye can reach as high as 50,000 feet. Wind speeds can exceed 155 miles an hour: Trees are toppled; roofs, windows, and doors are blown off; small buildings are leveled; and any structure less than 15 feet above sea level or less than 500 feet from shore is liable to be destroyed. Despite the high winds, much of the destruction of a hurricane results from abnormally high tides and from the wall of sea water that rides in as the storm approaches land. These hurricane waves can exceed 15 feet in height, and in coastal lowlands can cause damaging floods several miles inland. Torrential rains add to the flooding, washing out bridges, washing away towns and villages, and producing often devastating mud slides.

The most powerful hurricane ever to reach the Caribbean, Hurricane Gilbert, developed from a disturbance that formed in the Atlantic off the coast of Senegal. It was classified as a hurricane east of

Puerto Rico, and then struck Jamaica on September 12, 1988, with winds of 115 miles an hour. After leaving Jamaica it gained in strength, and when it arrived at Cancún at the tip of the Yucatán Peninsula two days later, its wind speed had increased to 175 miles an hour, with gusts of 218 miles an hour. When it finally crossed the coast of northern Mexico on the evening of September 16, its winds were down to 120 miles an hour, and by noon the next day, over the interior of Mexico, friction with the ground had reduced its wind speed by 80 percent. But its heavy rains produced record floods and spawned several tornadoes. With a wind speed of only 35 miles an hour, it no longer even qualified as a tropical storm, but it left a staggering 2,500-mile wake in which 750,000 people were homeless, at least 318 had lost their lives, and $5 billion in damage had been done.

The death toll from Hurricane Gilbert was small compared to the havoc wreaked in the days before hurricanes could be tracked by weather satellite, permitting these storms to strike without warning, giving coastal populations little chance to seek protection. In September 1938, a hurricane was detected

If a tree grows in the open, unprotected by surrounding trees, wind blowing against its great mass of foliage can snap it off near the ground.

(OPPOSITE): Testimony to the power of hurricanes: A 500-ton cargo ship (TOP) lies aground after the 1970 typhoon in Bangladesh. (BOTTOM): Waves spawned by Hurricane Flora (1963) crash against a lighthouse in Cuba.

Few weather events can match a tornado for sheer destruction. Here lies the remains of part of
Saragosa, Texas, after a twister in 1987.

Hurricane Hugo (OPPOSITE), later to devastate Charleston, South Carolina, lashes the trees at The
Bitter End, Virgin Gorda, in the British Virgin Islands, in September 1989.

north of Puerto Rico and seemed to be headed straight toward Miami. But it changed course, headed north over the Atlantic, and began to move remorselessly toward the northeastern United States. On September 21, the storm suddenly reappeared at Long Island's Westhampton Beach, with winds of 120 miles an hour and a 40-foot wall of sea water. The storm severely damaged the town of Westhampton; one man rode the roof of his house two miles inland before it finally came to rest. This hurricane cut a broad and devastating path across Long Island and New England. At Providence, Rhode Island, the water rose to 13 feet above the normal high-tide line. Forty-one people on the beach at Misquamicut, Rhode Island, were drowned before they had a chance to flee. On top of Mount Washington in New Hampshire, the wind was measured at 190 miles an hour. The total damage was estimated at more than $300 million, including the destruction of 26,000 cars, 3,000 acres of tobacco in the Connecticut Valley, and 4,500 buildings in southern New England alone. Before it weakened and ultimately died north of Montreal, this storm had killed 389 people.

Other storms have taken a toll even greater than that of the hurricane of 1938. The hurricane of September 12 to 17, 1928, plowed across the West Indies and into Florida, leaving 6,000 dead. In early October 1963, Hurricane Flora left 6,000 dead in Haiti and Cuba, and as recently as September 19, 1974, Hurricane Fifi hit Honduras, and more than 2,000 people lost their lives.

On November 13, 1970 (which happened to fall on a Friday), a tropical cyclone roared out of the Indian Ocean and up the valley of the Ganges River in Bangladesh, with winds of 120 miles an hour, torrential rains, and a tidal wave that killed more than 300,000 people, a third of whom were never found.

No wonder the word *hurricane*, which comes from the language of the Carib Indians of the West Indies, means "evil spirit." But sooner or later, even the most destructive of these storms grinds itself out over the interior of a continent, or heads out over cold ocean waters, where its energy is sapped and it finally dies.

The power of Hurricane Gilbert was the result of its unusual concentration. As it passed Jamaica, its eye was measured at only eight miles in diameter, less than a third that of a typical hurricane. The smaller the diameter of the center of any cyclonic storm, the faster its winds blow. The smallest cyclones have the most savage winds. These killer storms are tornadoes. Only a hurricane's greater size makes it more destructive. Tornadoes begin as violent swirls of air on the undersides of cumulonimbus clouds. These swirls are liable to form when two air streams with different temperatures, moisture content, and stability meet amid the turbulence of the air of a thunderstorm developing along a cold front. The spinning air forms a funnel and sometimes several, which may remain among the clouds. Sometimes the bottom of a cumulonimbus is studded with small, rounded protuberances—mammatocumulus—an ominous hint that tornadoes may be in the offing. If the wind causes one of these downward-pointing lumps to lengthen, it forms a white column of condensation that reaches down toward the ground. As long as it stays off the ground, it remains a beautiful if menacing white column, slowly turning, twisting, as if blindly feeling for something to touch. When it does strike the ground, its

In the wake of a winter storm at Benton Harbor on Lake Michigan, old-man's beard lichens hang frozen on trees along the shore (OPPOSITE). These hardy plants can survive such punishment.

(PAGES 136–137): The surf has been whipped up by a gale blowing more than 50 miles an hour.

appearance changes dramatically. The violent winds in the funnel begin to pick up dust and debris, and soon a mass of darker material rises from the base of the twister. In its worst stage, when it is doing its greatest damage, the white funnel of a tornado is completely obscured by a cloud of flying soil, leaves, branches, and even parts of houses. Those rare tornadoes that touch down on snow-covered ground remain white, although they too are quickly enveloped by a cloud of material from the ground. Once on the ground, tornadoes produce an indescribable roaring sound that is terrifying to hear. They cut a swath between 30 and 1,200 feet wide, and are often on the ground for less than 15 minutes before the funnel withdraws back into the clouds or dissipates.

Tornadoes are likely to occur in any region in which cold fronts and warm fronts collide. Ideal conditions occur on the Great Plains of North America, where polar air from Canada often meets warm air coming north from the Gulf of Mexico. Because of the frequency of collisions between this Canadian air and the warm Gulf air, the central United States has more tornadoes than anywhere else in the world—an average of 700 a year. Tornadoes are rare in the quiet air of equatorial regions, but are not uncommon in western Europe (where Britain alone has about 60 a year), in northern India, in Japan, and, in the southern hemisphere, in South Africa, Australia, New Zealand, and on the northern pampas of Argentina.

Much of the damage caused by tornadoes is the result of their intense winds, which often reach 300 miles an hour. In addition to flattening entire towns, these extraordinary winds can produce odd effects.

After a tornado has passed, pieces of straw are sometimes found embedded in telephone poles, tree branches may have pierced the walls of buildings, and splinters of wood can be driven through sheet metal. The very low air pressure in the center of one of these twisters—often less than 500 feet in diameter—is also a cause of much destruction: Sealed buildings can explode because of the greater air pressure inside them. One of the worst tornadoes on record was the killer storm that touched down in Missouri on March 18, 1925, and followed a 219-mile course through southern Illinois and into Indiana, leaving 695 dead and more than 2,000 injured. Another completely leveled the town of Udall, Kansas, on May 25, 1955, killing 80 people. Some storm systems spawn several tornadoes. The worst outbreak occurred on April 3, 1974, when 148 tornadoes twisted their way across 11 states, resulting in 329 deaths and more than $700 million dollars in damage.

All hurricanes spin cyclonically. Since they are tiny, intense cyclones, nearly all tornadoes follow this pattern as well. But for reasons meteorologists do not fully understand, an occasional tornado will spin clockwise in the northern hemisphere or counterclockwise in the southern hemisphere. It may be that its small size somehow frees it from the influence of the earth's rotation. There is much still to be learned about these most concentrated and deadly of wind storms. Their brief existence and their violence make them difficult to find and study.

Waterspouts are simply tornadoes that develop over water. Weaker than their mainland cousins, waterspouts have winds that rarely exceed 50 miles an

Still white, without having picked up any debris, a tornado snakes its way across the plains (TOP, LEFT). Another white tornado, this one in North Dakota, has begun to stir up debris at its base (TOP, CENTER); it gathers more flying debris (TOP, RIGHT; CENTER), and finally moves off, its harm done for the moment (BOTTOM).

In the flat pinelands of Michoacán, Mexico, where the soil is often loose and dry, a tall dust devil weaves its way among the trees.

Relatively harmless as long as it stays away from land, a waterspout crosses the water off the northwest coast of Puerto Rico.

hour. They are not as frightening as tornadoes, and can be exciting to watch from the apparent safety of the shore as they strike the surface of shallow, warm water and raise a great cloud of flying mist. But if a waterspout does happen to wander onto the land, it can be as destructive as a tornado. On February 7, 1971, a waterspout paid a brief visit to Pensacola, Florida, and did $3 million worth of damage.

Smaller still than tornadoes and waterspouts are dust devils, tiny spinning columns of sand and dust that rise from sun-heated ground, often carrying leaves and bits of paper aloft during their brief, swaying existence. Unlike a tornado, a dust devil is formed by heated air that rises from the ground, its spinning motion enhanced by local winds. Once it moves over cooler ground, it loses its source of energy and quickly dissipates, leaving paper, leaves, and dust to settle slowly back to the ground. Although dust devils are most common in deserts, they can be seen on any flat area of ground that is exposed to the sun.

Moist air rising over the Alps forms billowy orogenic cumulus clouds around the Matterhorn. If the winds are strong enough, these clouds may build to the point where they shed snow.

Fine sandstone, its layers delicately carved by dust and sand carried by the wind, is reflected in a pool among the arroyos of the Colorado Plateau (OPPOSITE).

Modern technology has harnessed the power of the wind to serve contemporary energy needs. (PAGES 144–145): Dozens of wind generators line the rolling landscape at Altamont Pass in California.

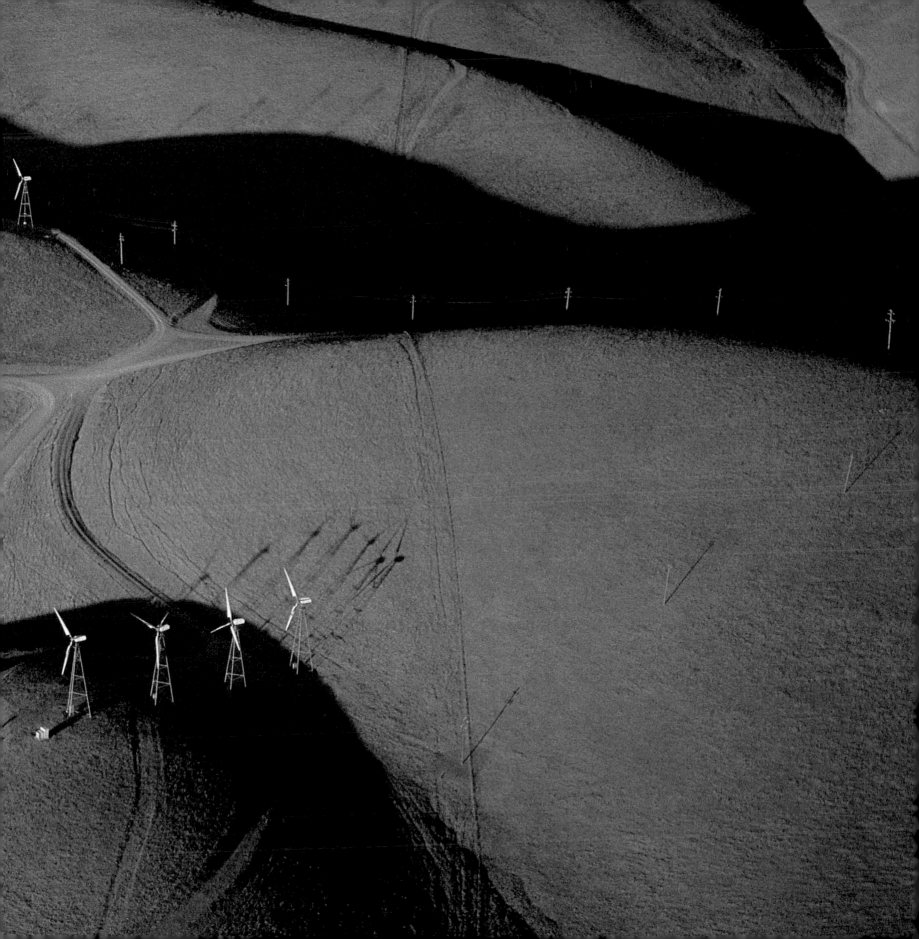

CHAPTER 7

UNDER SNOW OR RAIN: PRECIPITATION

IN JULY 1861, A BRITISH COLONIAL OFFICIAL WAS KEEPING records with a rain gauge at the little town of Cherrapunji, in the densely forested Khasi Hills of northeastern India's Meghalaya Province. It was the season of the monsoon, the steady southwesterly wind that blows ashore from the Indian Ocean during the summer and early fall. Here in the Khasi Hills, the first rampart of the mighty Himalayas, this wind begins to rise and shed the moisture it has carried all the way from the sea. The British agent had good reason to pay close attention to his rain gauge: In the previous eleven months he had measured what seemed, even in these wet hills, to be an unusual amount of rain. In that one month of July, more than 120 years ago, he measured a rainfall of just over 366 inches, or 30 feet, 6 inches. When he added this to the figures he had accumulated during the year beginning in August 1860, he found that he had measured 1,042 inches, or nearly 86 feet of rain. During that year, he established two records that still stand: the heaviest rainfall ever

measured in a single month, and the heaviest rainfall in a 12-month period. With rains such as this, it is perhaps no coincidence that the earliest known rain gauge—an ordinary bowl that caught rain as it fell—was in use in India by the fourth century B.C.

Nearly all of the rain at Cherrapunji falls between June and October. During the rest of the year, the monsoon wind blows from the northeast out of the dry interior of Asia, bringing hardly any rain at all. The year that ended in July 1861 was unusual even by Himalayan standards; despite their torrential rains and that record-breaking year, the eastern Himalayas are not the world's wettest place. That distinction belongs to the region with the greatest average annual rainfall, a place half a world away—the Chocó district on the Pacific coast of Colombia. There is no dry season in the Chocó. Here, warm, moist winds blow ashore all year long; when they meet the forested western slopes of the Andes they rise, producing rain almost continuously. The average rainfall in

A turbulent cumulonimbus prepares to bring a giant thunderstorm to Phoenix, Arizona.

A gentle morning mist rises slowly from the surface of Rose Lake in Minnesota (PAGES 148–149).
Because the mist has condensed in air chilled during clear, cold night, it is a good indication
that this day will bring no rain.

the entire Chocó is about 360 inches a year, and at Tutunendo, the annual average is 463 inches, or more than 38 feet, making this small Chocó town the wettest spot on earth.

Cherrapunji and Tutunendo owe their record-setting rains to the fact that local geography creates extreme examples of the conditions that produce all precipitation. In both places, a flow of moist air rises and cools, so that its moisture condenses, first as clouds, and then as rain. This is what lies behind the briefest of summer showers and the deepest of winter snows. In order for water to fall from the sky, it must first evaporate as water vapor, then rise, condense, and return to the ground.

Any one of several factors can cause moisture-laden air to rise. The air can be blown upward when winds encounter a mountain barrier, as they do in the Himalayas, the Colombian Andes, the Highlands of Scotland, or along the Northwest Coast of North America. It can be forced aloft when a cold front pushes its way beneath a mass of warmer air, or when a warm front flows up and over colder air. Moist air can also be lifted by the rising thermals that

precede and accompany thunderstorms, frontal cyclones, and hurricanes. Whether the water reaches the ground as rain, sleet, hail, or snow, or whether it reaches the ground at all, depends on what is happening in the atmosphere through which it falls.

In order for water vapor in chilled air to form droplets, it must condense around a nucleus, such as a bit of dust, a salt crystal, a pollen grain, a spore, or a particle of an air pollutant. As more and more water vapor attaches itself to the nucleus, the little mass of liquid water finally becomes heavy enough to begin its descent to the ground. In the higher reaches of the atmosphere, where the temperature is below freezing, all of the water is frozen; here, a tiny ice crystal provides a suitable nucleus.

Rain is the most common form of precipitation because most of the time the air close to the ground is above the freezing point. Even if water falls from a great height in the form of ice crystals, warmer air near the ground melts them and they arrive at the earth's surface as rain. The intensity of rain varies depending on the abundance of nuclei, the size of the raindrops, the height from which they fall,

A rainbow graces the Scottish Highlands as a long, gentle rain gradually comes to an end.

Lightning is nowhere more dangerous than at an oil refinery (OPPOSITE), but this one in Arizona is well protected by lightning rods and other forms of grounding from the crackling barrage that accompanies an arriving cold front.

and the amount of moisture in the air through which they pass. If there are many nuclei in the atmosphere, the raindrops are large, the cloud producing them is near the ground, and the air above the ground is moist, the resulting rainfall can be amazingly heavy. All of these conditions were met at Unionville, Maryland, on the Fourth of July in 1956, and 1.23 inches of rain fell in a single minute, a world record. In the town of Cilaos, on the slopes of Piton des Neiges on the island of Réunion in the Indian Ocean, 74 inches of rain fell on March 15 and 16, 1952; this torrential rain broke the record for a single 24-hour period, previously held by Baguio in the Philippines, the town that gave its name to the hurricanes that lash the region. Here, on a single day in July 1911, 46 inches of rain fell.

Rain must often fall from a great height or pass through dry air during its descent; the rain may evaporate before it reaches the ground. This can sometimes be seen as a virga, a wispy trail beneath a small cumulonimbus cloud. Virgas are especially likely to be witnessed in desert regions.

Between the extremes of cloudbursts and no rain at all is

drizzle, a fine, misty rain that falls or drifts from clouds so close to the ground that they have no time to grow into respectable raindrops. Drizzle is especially likely to occur when a thick stratus cloud moves in, obscuring the tops of buildings and hills and shedding its moisture off and on for days.

Sometimes rain falls from warm, moist air through a layer of cold air close to the ground. As they descend through the colder air, raindrops may freeze to any object they touch when they reach the ground. Such an ice storm, or glaze storm, leaves everything covered by a resplendent and dazzling coat of ice. Although beautiful, these are among the most destructive of winter storms. Roads acquire a slippery and dangerous coat of almost invisible "black ice," power lines fall under the weight of the glittering ice, and trees and their branches are splintered. A particularly severe ice storm struck Massachusetts in late November 1921, in which a layer of ice more than two inches thick developed, bringing down power lines and more than 200,000 trees; towns such as Worcester lost their electricity for several days.

If raindrops fall through a deep layer of cold air they may

These enormous hailstones fell on Fort Collins, Colorado, in the early 1980s, during a storm responsible for the destruction of car windows and property and even one death.

A huge, rain-bearing cumulonimbus (OPPOSITE) rises over the Arizona desert.

Ice storms are destructive both to wildlife and agriculture. (PAGES 154–155): A sudden freezing rain in early spring threatens to kill newly formed buds in a Michigan orchard.

turn into sleet—transparent ice pellets that have frozen before they reach the ground. This often happens when the temperature is hovering near the freezing point, making the ice pellets wet and slippery. Sleet may last only a brief time; a slight rise in temperature can cause ice pellets to change into a cold rain. To qualify as ice pellets, these bits of ice must be one-fifth of an inch or less in diameter.

This figure of a fifth of an inch is an important one, for it is the arbitrary measure that distinguishes ice pellets from hailstones. The descent of raindrops from the clouds to the ground is not always a simple one. In the turbulent air of a cumulonimbus, raindrops may fall for hundreds of feet, only to be caught in an updraft and blown upward to a level at which the temperature is below freezing. Here they freeze and begin to fall again. They may again be caught in an updraft and be hurtled aloft for a second time, when another layer of ice is added to their surface. This process can be repeated over and over, but finally these balls of ice, having developed concentric layers rather like those of an onion, become so heavy that no updraft can interrupt their fall to the ground. Because only a cumulonimbus provides the system of violent updrafts and downdrafts necessary for the formation of hail, hailstorms generally accompany these clouds and may be associated with tornados. Like raindrops, what are called the "embryos" of hailstones need a nucleus around which to form. Dust particles are the most common nuclei, but a hailstone that fell on Norman, Oklahoma, in June 1975 was found to have a tiny wasp as its nucleus.

Despite the fact that hail is made of ice, showers of hailstones often occur in warm weather. Hailstones usually form far aloft, in the freezing air at the top of a summer cumulonimbus, then fall through warm air without melting. The smallest hailstones are just over one-fifth of an inch in diameter, but those that have made many trips up and down before finally plummeting to earth can reach impressive sizes. The largest hailstone ever recorded weighed two and a quarter pounds, and fell on April 14, 1986, in Bangladesh. The hailstone holding the record for the United States fell on Coffeyville, Kansas, on September 3, 1970. It weighed 1.67 pounds and measured 7.5 inches in diameter.

Hailstorms like the one that hit Coffeyville can be highly destructive, killing people and livestock, devastating crops, smashing windows and piercing roofs, and battering aircraft that happen to fly through them. What was probably the world's worst hailstorm showered into the city of Moradabad in Uttar Pradesh, India, on April 30, 1888. Accompanied by a tornado, this storm killed more than 230 people, 200 of whom were struck down by hailstones. The boy who retrieved the Coffeyville hailstone was very sensibly wearing his football helmet.

Next to rain, the best-known form of precipitation is snow. While snow begins when water vapor condenses in the cold air at high altitudes, just as rain does, snowflakes freeze directly from water vapor into ice and usually encounter no warm air as they drift down from the clouds. In the northern hemisphere, snow develops most commonly near a low-pressure system, where warm, moist air passes around the center of the low and then rides up over the cold air that lies just to the north of the system. Since

Because it forms in thunderclouds, hail is as likely to fall in summer as at any other time of year.
In the Grand Canyon in June, a carpet of hailstones lies among the butterweed.

(PAGES 156–157): California's spectacular Yosemite Valley in winter.

the winds here are easterly, many snowfalls in the northern hemisphere arrive on an east wind.

Snowflakes begin as tiny, six-sided or six-pointed crystals of ice. It is these tiny hexagons that form the delicate cirrus clouds of high altitudes. If there is enough moisture in the air, the hexagons soon begin to grow at their six corners into the familiar lacy design of the classic snowflake. As they increase in size and weight, snow crystals start to fall from the clouds in which they form. Nearly anything can happen to a snowflake as it descends, and even the six-pointed crystal is almost endlessly variable. A snowflake can break, combine with other flakes, or pick up microscopic frozen droplets of water as it passes through a layer of altostratus. What arrives on the ground can look like a needle, a cube, a delicate prism, a six-sided cone, or a flat hexagon.

If a snowflake picks up enough frozen droplets on its way through an altostratus, it may arrive as a snow pellet, a pebble of snow less than one-fifth of an inch in diameter—smaller than a hailstone and differing from an ice pellet by being opaque and white, rather than transparent like a raindrop that has simply frozen during its descent. A snow pellet is firm enough to bounce when it strikes the ground rather than drift gently to rest. Snow pellets are sometimes called corn snow because they resemble white kernels of corn; meteorologists refer to them as graupel, their German name.

When moisture-laden winds flow up the slopes of mountains in the winter, the same conditions that produce record rains in warmer weather can produce record snowfalls. At the Paradise Ranger Station on the slopes of Mount Rainier in Washington State, where moist air from the Pacific Ocean ascends into the Cascade Mountains, the amount of snow that fell between February 19, 1971, and February 18, 1972, totaled 1,125 inches, or nearly 93 feet, the record for a 12-month period. The heaviest snowfall in 24 hours also occurred in the United States: 76 inches fell on April 14 and 15, 1921, at Silver Lake, Colorado.

These great snows did no harm because they fell quietly in remote, sparsely populated mountain regions. A more dangerous snowstorm can occur when even a modest snowfall combines with high winds. Although any heavy snow is likely to be

At the end of the day during the Great Blizzard of 1888, people braved the winds to walk home
from their work in Manhattan over the Brooklyn Bridge.

called a blizzard, this word really refers to paralyzing snowstorms accompanied by intense cold and gale-force winds that pile the snow into huge drifts.

The Blizzard of 1888 was such a storm. This greatest of all American blizzards really began as two storm systems, one born near Salt Lake City on March 8, the other a depression that formed in the southern states and began to move northward. The winter of 1887–1888 had been a severe one, but on Friday, March 9, the thermometer stood at 50°F (10°C). There was little to suggest what was in store for New York City and the rest of the Northeast as the southern storm became the major one. On the evening of Sunday the 11th, it reached New York City and rain turned to snow. During the night, the wind picked up, the temperature plunged, and the snow became heavier. By Monday morning, the wind was gusting to 84 miles an hour, bringing down most power lines in the city and cutting off normal communications. The blizzard lasted for more than 24 hours; snow accumulated at a rate of as much as an inch every hour for 20 hours. In some places in New York City, the gale blew a snowfall of only 20 inches into drifts 15 feet high.

In New Haven, Connecticut, the snowfall totalled 44 inches, and in nearby Middletown, it reached 50 inches, with huge drifts. The cities of the Northeast not only lost their telephone and telegraph communications with other cities, but all roads and trains were blocked by drifts. The first rescue trains made it through to New York on Wednesday the 14th, and by the following morning the temperature had risen above the freezing point. The great blizzard was over. In its wake, 400 people were dead, the majority victims of the intense cold who had been stranded in drifts or lost their way in the dense, flying snow, and seamen who had drowned in heavy and frigid seas just off shore.

Snow in mountainous regions can pose a threat of a different sort. All during the winter, snow accumulates on the cold heights. Triggered by wind, by the gradual melting that takes place in spring, or even by a sudden loud noise such as a rifle shot, an avalanche can bring an entire mountainside crashing down into the valley below it. On January 10, 1962, tons of ice and snow broke loose from the slopes of Huascarán in the Peruvian Andes and came thundering

New York's Madison Avenue after the Blizzard of '88 attests to the vast amounts of snow dumped on the city as well as to the wind's handiwork.

down onto mountain villages, where more than 3,000 people were buried. Even the wind produced by a descending avalanche can be deadly. In December 1952, when the wind that was pushed ahead of an avalanche came roaring down the Arlberg Pass—about 60 miles west of Innsbruck in the Lechtaler Alps of Austria—a bus carrying skiers was blown off a bridge; 23 of the 31 persons aboard perished.

Snow also has its lighter side. When snow that lies on a hill has melted a bit at its surface, the wind will sometimes cause the surface snow to peel away and roll down the slope, forming snow rollers, barrel-shaped masses of snow that grow as they move downhill. These snow rollers, which can also be seen on steep roofs, look as though they are the work of children who were about to build a snowman. Early settlers in North America spoke of snow fire, a dull red glow in the southwestern sky that often preceded a snowfall; in today's well-illuminated world, snow fire is seldom seen, but it does exist, a reliable sign of an approaching snowstorm that has never been satisfactorily explained.

Colored snowfalls can occur in southern Europe in the spring, when *simoom* winds blow dust from the Sahara across the Mediterranean. On March 9, 1972, Sahara dust containing copper salts mixed with snow falling in the Alps; the copper salts tinted the snow a pale blue. Other dust-filled winds from the Sahara have caused pink snowfalls in southern Europe. During the Dust Bowl in the 1930s, black snow fell in New York and Vermont. Rain, too, can carry colored dust: On April 9, 1970, Sahara dust produced a blood-red rain in Thessalonika in northern Greece. Such red rains have fallen as far north as Cornwall and Devonshire in England.

Both rain and snow feed the rivers and streams that water the earth. Here too, after they have completed their descent to the ground, they can create scenes of drama and destruction. No one knows for sure just what weather conditions produced the Deluge of the Bible—a flood that recurs in the tales of Native Americans, Australian Aborigines, and even the Fiji Islanders. But what happened in Florence in November 1966 was well documented and will long be remembered. It began as just another heavy rain, but quickly turned into one of the most famous and destructive floods of modern times. After a steady downpour during the night, the Florentines awoke on November 3 to find that the River Arno had overflowed its banks, and that their avenues and streets had become roiling torrents. The slopes of the mountains behind the city had long since been stripped of their forests, which might have held some of the water that now surged into the narrow bed of the river that courses through the city. The ground had already been saturated by heavy October rains.

On that November night, a mighty hydroelectric

When a dam along the Conemaugh River broke on May 31, 1889, Johnstown, Pennsylvania, suffered the worst flood in American history (OPPOSITE, TOP). Two days after the flood of November 1966, in Florence (BOTTOM), cars were still stranded in mud in front of the 13th-century Basilica di Santa Croce.

Fed by melting snow far upstream, the muddy waters of the Little Colorado River (PAGES 164–165) spill over fine layers of sandstone in northern Arizona.

dam 29 miles upstream, which had been designed to release water gradually, suddenly unleashed a huge wall of water. The reservoir behind another dam four miles downstream filled to overflowing almost instantly, and the engineers had no choice but to open the gates lest this lower dam give way under the burden and literally wash the city away. Instead, the river rose slowly but inexorably, spilling first over the south bank and then over the north, flooding the ancient medieval quarter and pouring into darkened houses and shops. More than 100,000 Florentines climbed to upper storeys or rooftops, where they were stranded all day and through the following night.

At seven in the morning on November 3, as the rains continued and water rose against the great doors of the Church of the Ognissanti, priests tried desperately to carry precious religious objects to safety, but finally the doors burst open with a crash and an oily brown surge of water swept into the nave, pushing a confused mass of chairs before it and drenching Botticelli's 15th-century fresco of St. Augustine. At the 13th-century Church of Santa Croce, the tombs of Galileo, Michelangelo, Machiavelli, and Rossini lay under 15 feet of water. The unrivaled collections of Etruscan art in the Museum of Archeology suffered irreparable losses. The floodwaters rose to the third floor of the Uffizi Gallery. More than a million priceless manuscripts and books in the Biblioteca Nazionale Centrale were buried under a deep layer of mud and slime. Thirty-five people drowned, and 15,000 cars were destroyed, but miraculously all of the bridges survived.

Never before had so much of the heritage of Western civilization been placed in such grave jeopardy.

The rain ended the following day, however, and within hours hundreds of scholars, artists, technicians, students, and ordinary citizens from all over the world began arriving in the stricken city to take up the monumental task of restoration. Today, almost a quarter of a century later, a visitor to Florence sees little or no evidence of this colossal disaster, but the work goes on. Behind the scenes, in the great palaces, churches, and museums, a multinational army is still painstakingly restoring the city of Dante, Leonardo, Michelangelo, and Raphael, and the birthplace of the oratorio, the piano, and the barometer, to its full glory.

In their gentler aspects, snow and rain are both cleansing and beautiful. A mantle of snow, cold as it is, protects small plants and animals beneath it from even harsher temperatures above. While dust from the Sahara may tint the snow with many shades, sunlight itself, playing over snow at dawn or dusk, can produce pink or blue shadows. Rain purifies the air, lulls us to sleep when it drums on the roof, nourishes crops, and releases a variety of delicate odors from the earth. Both rain and snow feed all rivers, and it is the rivers—even the Arno—that renew the fertility of the soil on which we grow our crops. However destructive they sometimes are, rain and snow are soothing just to watch, as raindrops dapple the surface of a pond or snowflakes settle peacefully onto the branches of evergreens. They are part of the ageless natural cycle of water on our planet—from the sea, to the sky, down to the ground and into rivers, and finally back into the sea. All creatures draw life-giving water from some point along this recurring circuit—a cycle of which we ourselves are a part.

Snow can be both problematic (OPPOSITE) and beautiful (PAGES 168–169).

(PAGES 170–171): The daily shower gradually clears as Guatemala's ancient, rain-washed pyramids of Tikal shine in the rays of the sun.

CHAPTER 8
SEA FOGS AND DUST STORMS: ATMOSPHERIC PARTICLES

AS THE DUKE OF CLARENCE LANGUISHES IN THE TOWER OF London in Shakespeare's *Richard III*, he complains that his soul is not free to find the "empty, vast, and wandering air." He has no way of knowing that while the air overhead is indeed vast and wandering, it is far from empty. Besides countless molecules of nitrogen, oxygen, argon, carbon dioxide, water vapor, and several other gases, the air contains larger particles, such as dust, bits of ash from forest fires and volcanoes, salt crystals, spores, pollen grains, droplets of water, and ice crystals. And today, nearly four centuries after Shakespeare wrote *Richard III*, a new class of particles—manmade pollutants—must be added to those that occur in nature.

It is, in fact, these molecules and particles that often give the sky its color. Longer waves of the sun's light, the reds and yellows, pass through the atmosphere, but the shorter blue waves are intercepted and scattered by the particles; it is this scattered, indirect light we see when we look up at the dome of the sky. A deep blue sky doesn't mean that there are no particles present, only that they are smaller. The purest blue skies are seen when particles are few and small—in the morning, in winter, over the ocean, and after a rain has cleansed the air of its larger particles. These last scatter more incoming light, creating a hazy, pale blue or whitish appearance. The sun usually looks yellow because the blue light is scattered, leaving only the longer yellow wavelengths to penetrate to the earth. The sky looks red or yellow at sunrise and sunset because sunlight has to travel on a slant through more of the atmosphere; the shorter, blue wavelengths are filtered out, and only the longer reds and yellows can reach the ground.

Although water vapor constitutes an average of only 1.4 percent of the air, it is the most important of the atmospheric gases in influencing weather. Cold air holds less moisture than warm air, and as the temperature drops, air gradually loses its ability to retain water vapor. This causes the air to become

After a major eruption, particles of volcanic ash can produce brilliant sunsets for months or years.

Along the Na Pali coast of the island of Kauai (PAGES 174–175), wisps of sea fog drift ashore and rise up the steep cliffs as sea air flows ashore to replace air that has warmed and ascended during the day.

saturated when it is cooled to the point of holding all the water vapor it can. Even a slight drop in temperature will then cause the vapor to condense into particles—droplets or ice crystals. The temperature at which this occurs is known as the dew point. Usually, this condensation takes place high above the earth's surface and results in clouds. But under a variety of conditions, the water vapor condenses at ground level rather than in the sky, and here the result is mist, if visibility is greater than about half a mile, or fog, if it is less.

The most common type of fog is formed on still, clear nights when the earth has radiated into space the heat it accumulated during the day, allowing the cooler ground to chill the air just above it. Fog formed in this way is most often seen the next morning as ground fog, or radiation fog—plumes of fog rising slowly from ponds, marshes, and wet meadows on an otherwise clear and sunny morning, or as patches of dense fog in the headlights of a car passing through a valley or ravine into which chilled air has flowed from higher ground nearby. Ground fog usually dissipates soon after the sun's rays warm the air again, and is generally a sign of clear weather. Valley fog forms during an inversion; the cool moist air in a valley is trapped under a layer of warm air, and because the heat and moisture cannot escape into space, a patch of fog develops. Like ground fog, valley fog usually disappears soon after sunrise.

Advection fog is produced when moist air flows over a colder surface, either on land or over water. In Maine, when a southerly wind blows in from warm, offshore waters, it passes over colder water near the coast, causing the water vapor in this maritime air to condense quickly. Such fog can be seen as a rapidly moving fog bank that obscures one island after another as it approaches the shore. Advection fog is common on the western coast of Europe and the Pacific Coast of the United States. In California, advection fog flows in off the ocean and over the hills that run along the coast. As the fog reaches the crests of hills, it is quickly burned off by the warm rays of the morning sun; wisps of fog can be seen spilling down the eastern slopes of the hills and vanishing before they reach the low ground just beyond. Advection fog can also develop under the opposite conditions: When cold air flows over a warm surface, moisture evaporating from the warm ground condenses in the chilled air above. Akin to advection fog is steam fog, or sea smoke—delicate wisps of fog that rise from the waves as cold air flows over warm water.

Wherever advection fog is a hazard to shipping, foghorns, usually at lighthouses on rocky promontories, warn ships when the fog has reduced visibility to about half a mile. Because humid air carries sound farther than dry air, it has been found that foghorns can be heard at greater distances during a uniform fog than they can when the air is clear. Even before fog develops, the sound of a foghorn carries farther, traveling through humid air that has not yet reached the dew point. But patchy fog is more dangerous. Sound bounces off the isolated areas of fog, sometimes causing ship captains to misjudge the position of a foghorn and the exposed rocks it warns of, increasing the risk of a shipwreck.

If air is forced up the slope of a mountain, it can chill as it ascends and form a layer of hill fog, or upslope fog, on the windward slope; such hill fog is common in

Ice crystals are often extremely beautiful, whether they are airborne (PAGES 176–177), **or stationary** (OPPOSITE).

the Pacific Northwest and in the Alps, but it sometimes forms a broad layer on the high plains of western Kansas and Colorado when a moisture-bearing wind from the Gulf of Mexico is cooled as it approaches the easternmost slopes of the Rocky Mountains. Still another fog—frontal fog—sometimes develops in advance of a warm front when rain falling through cold air ahead of the front forms a zone of small droplets near the ground.

On clear nights when there is not enough moisture in the air to form fog but objects on the ground are colder than the dew point, water vapor condenses as dew. When dew forms on clear nights, because there is no overcast sky to prevent the ground from cooling, it is usually a sign that good weather is ahead. Dewdrops usually collect when the temperature drops quickly just at sundown, and they survive until morning. If one walks across a dew-drenched lawn or meadow with the sun at one's back shortly after dawn, the dewdrops reflect back an image of the sun. The shadow of one's head then appears surrounded by a glow known as a heiligenschein, from the German for halo. More rarely, dewdrops act as tiny prisms that break the sunlight into multicolored rings around the shadow of one's head. This is called a glory, and is more commonly seen from the window of an airplane, around its shadow as it flies over a fog bank or cloud.

If the ground temperature is below freezing, moisture condenses as frost. In late fall and early winter in temperate regions, frost occurs most often in inland valleys where cold air flows down from surrounding hills. Later in the season, frost is likely to form anywhere, and if the air is charged with a great deal of moisture, large and beautiful ice crystals can form on branches, the bare ground, and on the inside of windows in moist rooms, where it forms delicate fernlike patterns. Like dew, frost forms more readily on clear nights because an overcast sky blocks escaping heat and enables the ground to retain its warmth.

Fog, dew, and frost all form from water vapor. Except for shipwrecks, rare now that most ships use radar for navigation, and traffic accidents caused when cars suddenly enter a patch of ground fog, water vapor and the droplets and frost crystals it forms are more beautiful than dangerous.

Other particles in the atmosphere can be more troublesome. The little dust devils that spin briefly across deserts and dry prairies are harmless enough, but dust storms are another matter. Except in the most barren of deserts, where most loose dust blew away ages ago, the roots of plants can usually hold down the soil. But after a prolonged drought, or when the soil has been disturbed by plowing or its plant cover removed by overgrazing, there is a risk of dust storms. On the southern margins of the Sahara, in the area known as the Sahel, native grasslands once supported prosperous tribes of herdsmen. Today, after years of drought, overgrazing, and the cutting of trees for firewood, this region has for all practical purposes become part of the Sahara itself. Entire populations have been forced to migrate southward, crossing political boundaries that have existed for scarcely a hundred years and moving onto land already inhabited by other tribes. Dust storms have produced famine and left a harsh, empty landscape where cattle-raising cultures had long flourished.

In a southern cypress swamp, a great egret (OPPOSITE, TOP) is seen through a dense ground fog.
(BOTTOM): A sudden chill causes moisture in the air to condense into a frost edging.

Fog in some of its forms: Ground fog (PAGES 182–183) in Glacier National Park, Montana;
advection fog over the Isle of Foula, Scotland (PAGES 184–185) and California's Golden Gate (PAGES 186–187).

Similar dust storms have afflicted India, and in centuries past so much dust has blown out of the Gobi Desert into the Pacific Ocean off China's coast that the waters off Jiangsu and Shandong provinces are called the Yellow Sea. But perhaps the most celebrated of all dust storms occurred on the Great Plains of North America. Here, native prairie grasses formed a thick sod that covered some of the most fertile soil in the world. But overzealous plowing, followed by a long dry spell in the early 1930s, created the Dust Bowl and caused severe dust storms that buried crops and houses and allowed millions of acres of valuable topsoil to blow away. Eyewitness accounts tell of great walls of reddish-brown dust that resembled moving hills, of blowing dust so thick that sunlight was completely obscured so that one couldn't see two feet ahead, and of drifts of dust more than 150 feet deep. Just as in the Sahel of Africa, this period of great dust storms caused a human migration. John Steinbeck's *Grapes of Wrath* portrays the plight of a dust-bowl family, one of the thousands that sought escape from their ruined farmland by migrating to California. Today, after the planting of grasses and cover crops to hold the remaining soil, the prairie states have recovered, but some experts predict another period of drought. Perhaps this land, fertile though it is, was never meant to be plowed. As long as humans turn the soil and expose it to the winds, another dust bowl remains an ominous possibility.

Dust storms can occur wherever soil is exposed to the wind. Sandstorms are generally born only in deserts. In spring in the Mediterranean region, a series of low-pressure systems moves from west to east, drawing the dreaded *simoom* winds out of the Sahara. Just as blinding as a dust storm, blowing sand is also abrasive, its larger and sharp-edged particles cutting into buildings and carving the surfaces of mesas and other rock formations. Whole towns can be buried under moving dunes, which a British meteorologist once described as "a sort of snow that never melts." The deserts of North America are too small to produce major sandstorms, but in the vast Gobi Desert, the worst are called *karaburan*, "black blizzards" that bury everything in their path. Unlike dust and ash, sand particles are heavy and fall back to earth

Far beyond a flat-topped acacia on the plains of Africa, a rainbow marks the place where a light shower is falling from a large cumulus cloud.

At dawn on a still, clear autumn day, every strand of a spider's orb web is bejeweled with drops of dew (OPPOSITE).

quickly, but the damage they do can be just as severe.

Other forms of dust and ash are sent into the atmosphere by volcanic eruptions. More than 500 volcanoes have erupted in historic times, and many of them have released great clouds of particles. On August 27, 1883, the dormant volcano Krakatau, between Java and Sumatra in Indonesia, suddenly exploded with great violence. More than 36,000 people drowned in the tidal wave that followed, debris fell 4,000 miles away on the island of Madagascar, and ships rocked at their moorings at Cape Town, 6,000 miles away. The shock wave circled the earth seven times in nine days, each time strong enough to be recorded by barometers in London. More than 10,000 miles away, in Hawaii, the sky was still white rather than blue ten days later because of all the volcanic ash thrown into the upper atmosphere, and for two years, sunsets around the world were brilliant red, indicating that the ash from this most colossal of modern eruptions still had not completely settled out of the atmosphere and back to the earth.

Forest fires are another major source of particles in the atmosphere. Smoke and fine ash pro-

duced as the flames roar through the trees are sent aloft by the heat of the fire itself, just as a thermal of warm air rises from ground heated by the sun. The smoke from a large fire can billow up like a cumulonimbus cloud, and at high altitudes the ash particles can provide nuclei for the formation of raindrops. Some forest fires actually bring rain down on themselves. But a major forest fire often survives a rainstorm. The flow of rising air can draw powerful winds inward toward the heart of the blaze, where they fan the flames and cause the fire to become even more destructive, just as the winds generated by fires during the heavy bombing of European cities in World War II caused savage fire storms that did more damage than the bombs. The great forest fire at Cloquet, Minnesota, on October 12, 1918, produced such strong winds that the wagons of firefighters were overturned and trees were snapped like matchsticks. More often, the smoke rises gently until it reaches a stable zone in the atmosphere. Here it spreads out and eventually drifts away on the wind. If a fire is large enough, the smoke may move downwind for thousands of miles. In late September 1950,

A dark wall of windblown dust and sand prepares to engulf a small Colorado town in 1956.

Along the arid Wadi Muhjeeb in the desert of Jordan, (OPPOSITE), windblown sand and dust have carved the cliffs.

Tiny ice crystals coat tree branches (PAGES 192–193) in Montana .

smoke from fires in northwestern Canada reached the Atlantic coast, where it tinted sunsets for days and even gave the midday sun a bluish cast.

Not all of the molecules and particles in the air are natural. Since the beginning of the industrial revolution, the burning of coal and other fossil fuels has sent an ever-increasing amount of carbon dioxide, methane, nitrous oxide, and chlorofluorocarbons into the atmosphere. This layer of "greenhouse gases" allows the heat of the sun to reach the surface of the earth, but then prevents much of it from escaping, just as the windows of a greenhouse keep plants warm in the winter. The longer wavelengths of the sun's radiation pass easily through this layer of gases, but the heat reflected back from the earth consists of shorter wavelengths, which cannot penetrate the layer and escape into space. Just as blue light is intercepted by particles in the atmosphere, the earth's shortwave radiation is intercepted by carbon dioxide and other gases in the atmosphere.

Steam and toxic chemicals pour into the air from an oil refinery in New Jersey.

(PAGES 194–195): Throughout the tropics, forest fires are sending tons of carbon dioxide into the atmosphere increasing the threat of climatic disruption by the greenhouse effect. In Cuba, for example, smoke from burning trees is tinted a deceptively attractive orange by the rising sun.

In the preindustrial age, the natural carbon dioxide in the atmosphere maintained a stable temperature balance on earth, but now that is changing. The result of this "greenhouse effect," most experts agree, will be a gradual warming of the earth's climate. It is estimated that the temperature will rise as much as 5°F (2.8°C) in the next 50 years. This change in temperature, at least ten times more rapid than that at the end of the last ice age, will make the earth warmer than it has been for 100,000 years and will cause major shifts in the world's climatic zones. In terms of weather, this change is expected to make storms more frequent and more powerful. In some regions, heat waves will be longer and more severe, while in others rainfall will be heavier.

Other manmade chemicals, among them sulphur dioxide, are now also in the atmosphere. From factories in North America and western Europe, and even from oil refineries in Mexico, smoke and chemical pollutants are being pumped into the atmosphere, where energy from sunlight causes chemical reactions; the pollutants return to the ground as acid rain, sterilizing lakes in the eastern United States, Canada, and Scandinavia, killing trees in Germany's ancient and beloved Black Forest, corroding the Lincoln Memorial in Washington and the great medieval cathedrals of Europe, and even corroding the monuments of Mayan civilization in the Yucatán and Guatemala. This is happening so fast that it has outstripped the ability of plants and animals to adjust to it in terms either of behavior or of evolution. How the planet's wildlife will deal with these rapid changes is difficult to predict, but without question many species are faced with extinction.

For countless centuries, the weather has operated just as it does now. It is only in this century that humans have come to understand how the weather really works. It is perhaps ironic that just as we have finally comprehended how and why our atmosphere behaves as it does, we are on the threshold of a change in our weather and climate that will tax our understanding as never before. The future of our own species, as well as of those others with which we share the earth, will depend on our ability to understand and cope with these changes.

Industrial pollution in Western Europe is damaging forests and acidifying lakes in Scandinavia, Germany, and Poland. Here smoke rises from the chimneys of a Welsh coal-mining town.

Among the historic monuments threatened by air pollution are the buildings on the Acropolis in Athens (PAGES 198–199), now necessarily marred by scaffolding as part of efforts to preserve them.

CHAPTER 9
RED IN MORNING, SAILOR'S WARNING: WEATHER FORECASTING

LONG BEFORE ARISTOTLE FOUNDED THE SCIENCE OF METE-orology, people were predicting the weather—making forecasts whose accuracy governed their success as hunters and gatherers, farmers, and seafarers. When Native Americans in the Northeast delayed their spring planting of corn until the oak leaves had grown to the size of a mouse's ear, or when ancient mariners saw a red sunset and knew the next day would bring good weather, they were acting on the accumulated wisdom of centuries. They may not have known how the weather works, but they knew to read the signs because both their lives and their livelihoods depended on it.

Virgil, who wrote the *Georgics* three centuries after the death of Aristotle, recorded some of the weather lore familiar to farmers in the Italian countryside:

Rain never catches men without some warning:
Either its surge has driven the skyey cranes
Before it down deep valleys, or a heifer

Looked up to heaven and spread her nostrils wide
To catch the breeze, or round and round the pond
The twittering swallow has flitted, and in the mud
The frogs have struck up their ancient croaking protest.

Just as much folk medicine has turned out to be based on the genuinely medicinal properties of plants, so modern science has explained the signs used in folk weather forecasting. We now know that the cause of red sunsets and sunrises is broken clouds that either follow or precede stormy weather. When a storm is departing, broken clouds behind it—to the west—permit some rays of sunlight to shine through the lower atmosphere. All but the red rays are absorbed by haze or polluted air, so that the clouds have a red color. The same thing happens at sunrise when broken clouds lie to the east, ahead of the bad weather, and solid banks of clouds, which will soon cover the whole sky and perhaps bring rain, lie to the west.

A hot-air balloon ascends in the cool air of dawn. Though not a weather balloon, its movements will still reveal something about the changing direction of the wind high above the ground.

(PAGES 202–203): Not all rain forests are in the tropics. At Glacier Bay National Park in Alaska, about 200 inches of rain fall every year; tree trunks, branches, and the ground are covered with a lush growth of mosses and ferns.

Modern weather forecasting is based both on local observations of weather conditions made by weather stations joined together in a worldwide network and on information recorded by satellites orbiting the earth. Weather prediction relies on the gathering of readings of local temperature, atmospheric pressure, relative humidity, wind direction and speed, and amount of precipitation. To take these readings, a variety of instruments are used—some hundreds of years old; all with modern improvements.

In the recording of weather conditions and in forecasting, the three basic measurements are those of temperature, atmospheric pressure, and relative humidity. Temperature readings are usually taken with sealed tubes that contain a liquid, generally mercury or alcohol. As the temperature rises, the liquid expands, causing it to rise inside a tube marked in degrees Fahrenheit or Celsius; with a drop in temperature, the liquid contracts and is drawn back down the graduated tube. Although such thermometers react continually to changing temperatures, they are also capable of recording their maximum temperature readings by trapping some of the liquid at the uppermost point it reaches. A minimum temperature reading is preserved in a horizontal alcohol thermometer that contains a small glass "index." As the liquid contracts, the index is drawn along the tube by capillary action, but when the temperature rises again and the alcohol expands, the vessel is stranded at the point of the lowest reading.

Bimetal thermometers contain coiled strips of two different metals. Since the two metals expand and contract differently as the temperature rises and falls, a change in temperature causes the coil to change its curvature; a needle attached to the coil then moves along a scale. Electrical thermometers depend upon the fact that the electrical conductivity of metals changes as the temperature rises or falls. Such thermometers can transmit their readings over long distances as radio signals, making them ideal to measure temperatures at high altitudes.

Because direct sunlight can warm any thermometer to a temperature above that of the air around it, thermometers must always be kept in sheltered places. A thermometer should also have air circulating freely around it because motionless, or "dead," air can have a different temperature than that of moving air. Thermometers are usually kept in an open spot, covered by a wooden, boxlike shelter with overlapping slats that keep sunlight out but allow air to pass through the interior of the box. Fortunately, the windchill factor—the cooling effect of the wind—is only felt by the human body and does not change the readings of thermometers. Even with all these precautions, however, small local effects, such as sunlight striking a nearby patch of ground, can alter a temperature reading; therefore, at least for thermometers on the ground, readings are generally considered to have a margin of error amounting to a degree or two.

Since changes in atmospheric pressure accompany

During much of the year, the tundra on the Alaska Peninsula is bleak, cold, and dry. But during the brief arctic summer, when water from melting ice forms a vast plain of bogs and marshes, the landscape becomes as green as anywhere on earth.

(PAGES 206–207). Washington State's frost covered Olympic National Park.

(PAGES 204–205): Once a scene of fiery volcanic upheaval, the Katmai region of Alaska is now a silent, icy wilderness. But after its 1918 eruption, a foot-deep layer of ash particles covered Kodiak Island, 100 miles away.

the arrival and departure of high- and low-pressure systems, barometers, especially when readings are tallied from many different points, tell much about the nature of impending weather. A barometer is really an instrument for measuring the weight of the air above it and, when a large and relatively heavy "pile" of air in the midst of an air mass lies over a barometer, it records a high pressure. During the passage of a depression there is less air above the barometer, and so it gives a lower reading.

The mercury barometer is a tube of glass with one end sealed and the other inserted in a cup of mercury. As the weight of the air above increases, the mercury is forced back in the tube until the weight of the mercury equals that of the air. Readings of the height of the column of mercury in the tube, often in inches, are then taken. A barometric pressure of about 30 inches is normal at sea level. If the readings begin to drop, we know that the atmospheric pressure is falling—a sure sign that a depression is on its way and that we can expect cloudy or wet weather.

A tube of mercury, although very accurate, is somewhat inconvenient to carry around,

making the aneroid barometer very useful. This instrument is a thin metal chamber with most of the air removed. As the amount of air above the barometer increases, the chamber, which encloses a partial vacuum, contracts under the pressure of the air. A spring prevents the chamber from collapsing, and if it is attached to a needle that moves along a scale, readings of the atmospheric pressure can be obtained. Like electrical thermometers, aneroid barometers can be connected electrically so that their readings can be sent long distances. Aneroid barometers are less accurate than mercury barometers, but because they can transmit data and can't spill mercury, they are used in weather rockets and as altimeters for mountain climbers.

The amount of water vapor in the air is important in weather prediction because it is the source of the moisture from which rain and snow develop. The content of water vapor in the atmosphere varies from nearly 0 percent to about 4 percent. The more water vapor there is in the air, the harder it is for water to evaporate; when the air is saturated (at

Although the sky has become overcast, these giant sunflowers in South Dakota still face in the direction in which the sun was last visible.

the dew point), no water can evaporate, and fog or dew may develop. Relative humidity, which influences how uncomfortable we feel on hot, humid days, is the ratio between the amount of water vapor in the air and the amount there would be at the dew point, when the air would be saturated. This measurement is expressed as a percentage; a relative humidity of 100 percent means that the air is saturated.

The most common instrument used in determining relative humidity consists of two ordinary, sealed thermometers. The bulb of one thermometer—the "wet bulb"—is wrapped in wet cloth. The other "dry bulb" is not wrapped, and records the air temperature. As water evaporates from the wet bulb, it cools that thermometer, recording a lower temperature than the dry bulb. The difference between the readings of the two thermometers tells how much water vapor is in the air: In dry conditions, the wet bulb cools rapidly, while at the dew point no evaporation is possible. With these two readings and the difference between them, the relative humidity and the dew point can be determined by consulting appropriate tables.

Another instrument used for

obtaining the relative humidity—the electrical hygrometer—consists of a metal electrical conductor coated with lithium chloride, a substance that readily absorbs water. The amount of water absorbed changes the amount of electricity the metal can conduct. Because this change in conductivity can be sent long distances by radio, this instrument accompanies electrical thermometers and aneroid barometers in rockets or balloons sent into the atmosphere. Such a balloon equipped with its instruments and radio transmitter, is called a radiosonde, and is a valuable apparatus for studying the weather at high altitudes.

Determining the direction and speed of the wind is much easier. A simple weather vane, such as those farmers have placed on their barns for centuries, points in the direction from which the wind is blowing; a "northwest" wind, for example, is blowing from the northwest rather than toward it. The speed of the wind is measured with a cup anemometer, a pole with several cups attached to it. Air striking the concave sides of the cups causes them to spin; the speed at which they spin is then translated into miles per hour or knots. Measuring wind conditions at

A light, wet snowfall has coated every twig of this sugar maple.

high altitudes involves helium-filled balloons, which are sent up and then watched either by eye or with radar. The movements they make provide a simple way of determining both the direction and the speed of winds high above the ground. Many weather balloons carry radio transmitters with them, and can quickly send their data back to a weather station.

Modern rain gauges are merely sophisticated versions of the simple bowl used in India in the fourth century B.C. A cylinder, usually fitted with a funnel, is marked off in inches or centimeters. After a rain, the level of the water in the cylinder tells how much rain fell on an area the size of the mouth of the funnel. The standard rain gauge of the U.S. Weather Service has a funnel with a diameter of eight inches, or an area of just over 50 square inches. The amount of rain falling on this area is measured with a calibrated wooden stick inserted into the cylinder.

The depth of a snowfall is important because the snow may remain on the ground for some time, later serving as a reservoir of water that feeds into streams at the end of a cold spell or in the spring. Measurements are usually taken with a fixed gauge planted in the ground. Converting a reading of snow depth into

Bringing moisture all the way from the Pacific Ocean, a cloud spills over the Continental Divide in Glacier National Park. Beyond these peaks, rain is probably falling.

the equivalent amount of water is tricky because the size and compactness of snow vary so much; in general, ten inches of snow is equivalent to one inch of rain. For exceptionally loose snow, the conversion may be up to 20 inches of snow per inch of water.

All of these measuring devices have been in use for centuries. Today, the information they provide is assembled from hundreds of weather stations and is used to form a comprehensive picture of the weather over wide areas, both at ground level and in the upper reaches of the atmosphere. The data gathered can be put into a computer and the movements of weather systems plotted and predicted. Radar stations can track rainstorms, snowfall, clouds, and dust storms, telling instantly where a weather system is, what kind of precipitation it is producing, where it is heading, and how fast it is moving. Weather satellites orbit the earth and send back photographs of cloud patterns, as well as of areas of the earth's surface experiencing solar heating, enabling us to track major storms with an accuracy that will prevent a repetition of the sneak attack visited on Long Island and New England by the great hurricane of September 1938. Long before a tropical disturbance has acquired the appearance of a dense, circulating mass of white clouds in the doldrums, a satellite has spotted it, and its movements and behavior are being studied.

With this array of equipment at its disposal, and with experts watching the sky from the ground and making observations and measurements from aircraft, the National Weather Service, an arm of the National Oceanic and Atmospheric Administration (NOAA), collates all of this information and prepares the computer models and forecasts used in agriculture and industry, and by the general public. Modern weather forecasts are made by using a technique known as numerical prediction. With mathematical equations and computers that can make millions of high-speed calculations, future weather conditions are projected on the basis of the temperature, air pressure, wind speed, relative humidity, and other variables at a given moment. Such a projection is used in turn to project the weather at a time still farther in the future. Although numerical weather prediction relies on a large amount of data, many weather phenomena have life spans of only a few days, which makes the accuracy of projections decrease as they are pushed farther into the future. But such computer projections are our best means of predicting the weather, as good as or better than predictions made by the most experienced human forecaster.

The "vast and wandering air" is really a fluid in motion, and such a large number of variables can act upon it that no mathematical equation or computer model can predict every weather situation that might occur. More and more, people are speaking of the "science of chaos," a new field of research into the behavior of fluids in motion. This expression aptly conveys the difficulty of trying to tell what our complex, ever-changing atmosphere will do next.

NOAA Weather Radio, the source of weather reports given by other radio stations, by television stations, and by newspapers, broadcasts weather reports 24 hours a day on nearly 400 FM stations in the United States. These stations provide detailed local weather information for about 90 percent of the United States and include both coastal and offshore waters in their coverage. Another 15 stations broadcast on the same frequencies in southern Canada.

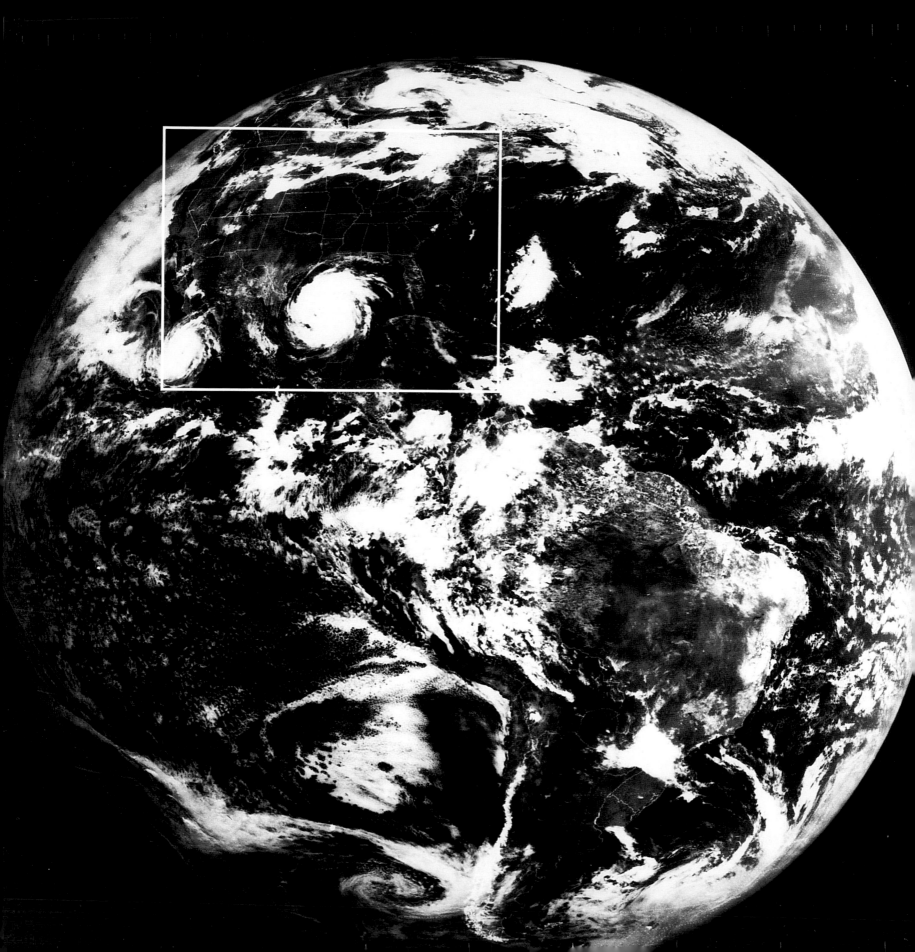

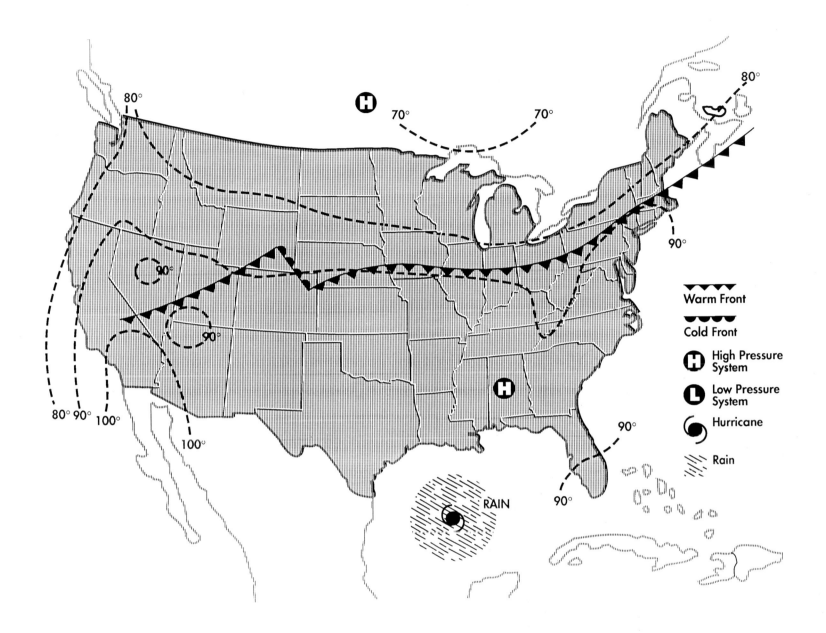

Warm Front

Cold Front

H High Pressure System

L Low Pressure System

Hurricane

Rain

Two ways of viewing the weather of August 8, 1980: A weather map (ABOVE), which details the inset
on the NASA satellite photograph (OPPOSITE). As Hurricane Allen approaches the Texas coast,
a high-pressure system is stalled over the Southeast, and a long cold front stretches across the
United States. A warm front is moving northeast over Wyoming,
where a low-pressure system will soon develop.

(PAGES 216–217): Tropical vegetation gets a thorough drenching of warm rain on the Hawaiian
island of Oahu.

Weather maps are also useful in learning about the weather. Most newspapers print weather maps every day, and while they vary from simple to complex, none are difficult to read. By saving them it is possible to keep a record of a front or low-pressure system as it moves across the country, and observation of maps over time shows how the jet stream guides storms along its eastward path. Armed with a set of weather maps and the broadcasts of NOAA Weather Radio, one can keep track of the weather, a pursuit that for some can be as absorbing as following major-league baseball or professional football.

But in the end, there is no substitute for going out and watching the weather itself. Very soon, you will see good examples of all ten of the major types of clouds, and by noting the direction in which they are moving, you will soon come to understand what is happening overhead, and why. An inexpensive thermometer, barometer, and weather vane will add to the information easily observed. Many weather watchers keep an informal journal, recording their own observations as well as the weather data printed

A rain storm sweeps across the dry, flat terrain of southern Arizona.

in newspapers or reported on television and radio.

Today, most of us live in a world where local weather events are interesting or, at worst, inconvenient. Seldom do they pose a threat to our homes, our sources of food, or our lives. Even though the weather is still sometimes unpredictable, and forecasts sometimes wrong, this rarely means more than being caught without an umbrella. But we have lost touch with the natural world and have forgotten the weather lore used by our ancestors, just as we have forgotten much of what they knew about the plants and animals around them. Instead, we rely on forecasts made possible by a worldwide network of data-collecting stations that transmit weather information to us via the media. Like wildlife, weather is part of the natural world, a world we rarely see close up in this mechanized age. But the ancient weather signs are still there, and those who learn to read them can experience nature firsthand.

Torn by the wind, an orographic stratus cloud slides over Minerva Spring in
Yellowstone National Park.

(PAGES 220–221): Probably triggered by a cumulus cloud that built up over the high mountains, a
thunderstorm moves over Yellowstone National Park in Wyoming.

Appendices

A. Signs of Weather from Animals and Plants

The behavior of animals and plants has always been considered a source of information about the weather. Among many bits of folklore, the following have been shown to be trustworthy weather signs.

SNOWY TREE CRICKETS

The snowy tree cricket is a pale-green insect that is common everywhere in the United States except the southeastern states. Like all insects that have calls, the rate at which this pale-green, tree-dwelling species produces its mellow rhythmic sounds in late summer and fall decreases as the temperature lowers. One can use this fact to make a rough reading of the temperature. Take the number of calls per minute, divide it by four, and add 40. The result will be the approximate temperature in degrees Fahrenheit. A quicker method to obtain this reading is to count the number of chirps in 14 seconds and add 40.

RHODODENDRON LEAVES

At normal temperatures, the leaves of rhododendrons are upright and held horizontally. If the temperature drops to 35°F, the leaves begin to droop and curl, at 32°F they hang downward, and at 20°F they hang downward and are tightly curled.

DANDELIONS

Dandelions bloom from early spring until late in the fall. At normal temperatures their flowers are open, but if the thermometer dips below 51°F their flowers close.

CICADAS

These common insects call from trees on warm sunny days in summer. They are sensitive to moisture in the air and if the relative humidity drops suddenly during a rainstorm, they will abruptly start calling, an indication the rain is about to end.

SCARLET PIMPERNEL

This common plant closes its flowers if the relative humidity rises to about 80 percent, and thus protects its pollen from rain.

COCKROACHES

These household pests react to sudden drops in atmospheric pressure. If you see cockroaches running around in broad daylight, it is an indication that a large low-pressure system, perhaps even a hurricane, is about to arrive.

GULLS

Gulls are living weather vanes. Whenever a flock of gulls rests on a sandbar or pier, they face into the wind in order to avoid ruffling their feathers.

B. THE BEAUFORT SCALE

In 1806, when ships sailed under canvas, Captain Beaufort of the British Royal Navy devised a simple means of estimating the speed of the wind by observing its effects on the sea and on objects on land. By the time of his death in 1857, Rear Admiral Sir Francis Beaufort had seen his scale adopted by the British Admiralty for all of its ships at sea, but he didn't live to see it accepted by the International Meteorological Committee for reporting wind speeds worldwide. Although his scale has partly been supplanted by modern wind-measuring instruments, it is still useful both on land and on the sea. In its present form, the Beaufort Scale contains 13 divisions.

CODE NUMBER	WIND SPEED (MPH)	DESIGNATION	DESCRIPTION
0	Less than 1	Calm	Smoke rises vertically; sea mirror-calm
1	1–3	Light Air	Wind direction indicated by smoke but not by weather vane
2	4–7	Light Breeze	Wind felt on face; direction indicated by weather vane; leaves rustle
3	8–12	Gentle Breeze	Wind extends light flags; leaves and twigs in constant motion; small crests on waves
4	12–18	Moderate Breeze	Dust and loose paper raised; small branches move; wave crests begin to break
5	19–24	Fresh Breeze	Small trees sway; wave crests form on inland waters
6	25–31	Strong Breeze	Large branches move; wind whistles in wires; umbrellas difficult to handle
7	32–38	Moderate Gale	Whole trees move; walking inconvenient
8	39–46	Fresh Gale	Twigs break off; walking difficult
9	47–54	Strong Gale	Slight structural damage occurs; foam streams from wave tops
10	55–63	Whole Gale	Trees uprooted; considerable structural damage; waves huge, with overhanging crests
11	64–74	Storm	Widespread damage
12	75+	Hurricane	

GLOSSARY

Acid Rain   Rain containing corrosive acids such as sulphuric acid, formed by the oxidation of sulphur dioxide, a common industrial pollutant.

Advection fog   Fog produced either when warm, moist air is chilled as it flows over cold land or water causing its water vapor to condense into particles of water, or when cold air flows over warmer land or water and moisture evaporating from the warm surface condenses in the chilled air above.

Air mass   A large body of air, often covering hundreds or thousands of square miles, whose temperature and humidity are relatively uniform at any given altitude.

Altocumulus   A middle cloud consisting of a layer of small cloudlets, formed by turbulence; they often have darkened undersides but usually transmit sunlight.

Altocumulus castellanus   An altocumulus cloud with small towers that are produced by currents of air rising from the cloud's interior; usually an indication of unstable air.

Altocumulus translucidus   A thin layer of altocumulus that transmits much of the sun's light.

Altostratus   A middle cloud that consists of a thick, uniform layer that usually blocks the light of the sun but is high enough to cast no shadow. Altostratus sometimes grades into a nimbostratus cloud.

Aneroid barometer   A barometer in which the pressure of the atmosphere on a thin sheet of metal causes a needle to move along a gauge.

Anticyclone   A high-pressure system with winds circling it clockwise in the northern hemisphere and counterclockwise in the southern hemisphere.

Arctic (Antarctic) semi-permanent high   A high-pressure system lying almost constantly over the poles; the winds blow clockwise around the Arctic semi-permanent high and counterclockwise around the Antarctic semi-permanent high.

Atmosphere   The layer of nitrogen, oxygen, and other gases surrounding the earth.

Atmospheric pressure   The downward force of the air over a particular area, averaging 14.7 pounds per square inch at sea level.

Barometer   An instrument for measuring atmospheric pressure.

Bimetal thermometer   A thermometer in which two attached strips of different metals, each of which expands at a different rate when heated, bend and cause a needle to move along a gauge.

Blizzard   A snowstorm characterized by subfreezing temperatures and high winds, in which large drifts of snow often form.

Bora A cold winter wind that blows down from the Alps into the Adriatic Sea, bringing low temperatures, heavy seas, and snow to Italy and Yugoslavia.

Chinook A strong, dry wind that is warmed as it flows onto North America's Great Plains from the Rocky Mountains, often causing the temperature to rise dramatically in a few minutes.

Cirrocumulus A high cloud that consists of a thin layer of white ice crystals broken into bands or rows of small tufts by rising currents of air. Like other high clouds, cirrocumulus contains no shadows.

Cirrocumulus undulatus A sheet of cirrocumulus with waves or undulations produced by the wind.

Cirrostratus A high cloud that consists of a gray or white, translucent layer of ice crystals.

Cirrus A delicate, wispy or fibrous cloud formed by high-altitude winds; often called mare's tails. Like other high clouds, cirrus is composed of ice crystals and is too thin to have shadows.

Cold front The leading edge of a moving air mass that is colder than the one it is replacing. Such fronts usually travel more rapidly than warm fronts, and are often accompanied by brief, heavy rain.

Coriolis force A force that is produced by the rotation of the earth and that deflects the path of moving objects to the right in the northern hemisphere and to the left in the southern hemisphere. The coriolis force causes weather systems to move in a generally easterly direction in both hemispheres.

Cumulonimbus A very large, thick cloud, formed by strong thermals of moist, rising air, and often reaching a height of 12 miles, where the jet stream shears off its top and gives it the shape of an anvil. A cumulonimbus cloud produces heavy rain and thunderstorms. Also called a thundercloud.

Cumulus A small, compact, white cloud with a rounded top and a flattened bottom, formed at the top of a rising thermal of moist air, and classified as a vertical cloud.

Cumulus congestus A large, white, billowing cloud, dark on the bottom and with high peaks and troughs on its top; formed by the enlargement of a cumulus cloud.

Cumulus mammatus A cumulus cloud with small protuberances on its underside, produced by turbulence in the air beneath it, and often formed in association with thunderstorms. Also called mammatocumulus.

Cup anemometer An instrument that carries cups that, by turning when the wind blows, measure wind speed.

Cyclone A low-pressure system with winds circling it

counterclockwise in the northern hemisphere and clockwise in the southern hemisphere; the name given to hurricanes in the Indian Ocean.

Dew Droplets of water formed when moisture in the atmosphere condenses on contact with cool objects.

Dew point The temperature at which the air is cooled to the point where the water vapor in it condenses.

Doldrums A zone of low pressure, high humidity, and calm winds on either side of the Equator.

Drizzle A fine rain produced by low-lying clouds, with droplets just heavy enough to fall or drift toward the earth.

Dust devil A small, temporary vortex of rising dust and air, caused by solar heating of the ground.

Dust storm A large wind storm carrying clouds of dust and other fine particles.

Electrical hygrometer An instrument that measures the amount of moisture in the air by recording the rate of electrical conductivity in a coating of lithium chloride, a substance that absorbs water; the rate of conductivity changes with the amount of moisture absorbed.

Electrical thermometer An instrument that measures temperature by recording the rate of electrical conductivity in a metal; the rate of conductivity changes with the temperature.

Foehn A dry mountain wind that is liable to descend from the Alps at any season.

Fog A mass of particles of water floating in the air near the ground, in which visibility is less than about half a mile. Cf. Mist.

Freezing rain Rain that turns to ice on contact with cold objects.

Front The leading edge of a moving air mass.

Frontal cyclone A cyclone formed along a front when the front lies beneath a trough in the jet stream and the flow of air around the trough produces a counterclockwise circulation of air near the ground.

Frontal fog Fog that develops in advance of a warm front, when rain falling through cold air ahead of the front forms a zone of small droplets near the ground.

Frost Crystals of ice formed when moisture in the atmosphere condenses and freezes to cold objects.

Glory A multicolored ring or halo seen around the shadow of an airplane or an observer's head when droplets of water in a cloud or dewdrops in the grass act as prisms that reflect sunlight just as a rainbow does. Also called a heiligenschein.

Graupel   *See* **Ice pellet.**

Greenhouse effect   A predicted warming of the climate of the earth, caused by increasing amounts of carbon dioxide and other gases, which will permit solar heat to enter the atmosphere but then, like the glass in a greenhouse, prevent it from escaping back into space.

Ground fog   Fog formed on clear nights when the earth radiates its heat into space and the cold ground chills the air just above it. Such fog is often seen early in the morning, just before the heat of the sun causes it to evaporate. Also called radiation fog.

Hailstone   A solid, layered ball of ice formed when a droplet of water or bit of ice rises and falls in the turbulent interior of a cumulonimbus cloud, on each descent collecting a coat of water that then freezes on the following ascent. Before it finally reaches the ground, a hailstone may grow to several inches in diameter.

Heiligenschein   *See* **Glory.**

High clouds   Clouds that form 6 or 7 miles above the ground, and are usually composed of ice crystals. Cirrus, cirrocumulus, and cirrostratus are the principal high clouds.

High-pressure system   An area of high atmospheric pressure, usually characterized by clear skies and an absence of precipitation. Often called an anticyclone.

Hill fog   Fog formed when moist air is forced up the slope of a mountain and is chilled as it ascends, causing the water vapor to condense into droplets of water.

Horse latitudes   A zone of calm air and little wind lying at about 35 degrees north or south of the Equator.

Hurricane   A cyclone formed over warm water near the Equator, whose wind has reached a speed of at least 75 miles an hour.

Ice pellet   A raindrop that has frozen into a glassy, transparent pellet of ice, less than one-fifth of an inch in diameter, and lacking the layered structure of a hailstone.

Ice storm   *See* **Freezing rain.**

Isobar   A line on a weather map joining points at which the atmospheric pressure is the same. Isobars form circles around many low-pressure systems.

Jet stream   *See* **Subtropical jet stream; Westerly jet stream.**

Lenticular cloud   A stationary, often lens-shaped cloud formed over a mountain or downwind from it, when a flow of moist air rises high enough for its moisture to condense, and then sinks back into a warmer layer where the moisture evaporates again. Also called a wave cloud.

Low clouds   Clouds that usually form less than three miles above the ground, and are generally composed of droplets of water. The principal low clouds are stratus, stratocumulus, and nimbostratus.

Low-pressure system   An area of low atmospheric pressure, usually accompanied by circling winds, clouds, and precipitation. Often called a cyclone.

Mackerel sky   A sky with clouds showing the patterned structure of altocumulus.

Mammatocumulus   *See* **Cumulus mammatus.**

Mare's tails   *See* **Cirrus.**

Mercury barometer   A barometer in which the pressure of the atmosphere forces a column of mercury to move up a calibrated tube.

Meteorology   The science that deals with atmospheric phenomena and the weather.

Middle clouds   Clouds that form between 15,000 and 20,000 feet above the ground, and are composed either of ice crystals or droplets of water. The principal middle clouds are altocumulus and altostratus.

Mist   A mass of particles of water floating in the air near the ground, in which visibility is greater than about half a mile. *Cf.* Fog.

Mistral   A cold, violent wind that blows out of the Alps and is funneled down the valley of the Rhône.

Monsoon   Either of two seasonal winds: (1) a dry northeast wind that blows into the Indian Ocean from Siberia during the winter; and (2) a moist southwest wind that blows from the Indian Ocean into the Himalayas during the summer, bringing drenching rains to the mountain slopes. Other pairs of seasonal winds are sometimes called monsoon winds.

Nimbostratus   The largest of the low clouds; a very thick, uniformly dark-gray layer that usually accompanies a low-pressure system or front, and produces sustained rain or snow.

Norther   A sudden cold spell on the Great Plains, produced by the arrival of a Polar Continental air mass from Canada in winter.

Occluded front   A front formed when a cold front overtakes a warm front. Along an occluded front, warm air is lifted above the ground and may shed rain or snow for some time.

Prevailing westerlies   Winds that blow mainly from the west, between 35 and 60 degrees north and south of the Equator. *See also* **Roaring Forties.**

Radiation fog   *See* **Ground fog.**

Rain gauge   A device or instrument for measuring the amount of rainfall at a given place and time.

Relative humidity   The amount of water vapor in the air, expressed as a percentage of the amount there would be at saturation, given the temperature.

Ridge   A zone of high atmospheric pressure lying beneath a northward bend in the westerly jet stream, where the wind is blowing anticyclonically.

Roaring Forties   The zone of prevailing westerly winds lying between 35 and 60 degrees south of the Equator, where the absence of land masses allows strong winds to blow almost constantly.

Sandstorm   A large wind storm carrying clouds of sand and other coarse particles.

Sirocco   A hot wind that blows into the Mediterranean region from the Sahara in the spring, carrying dust to southern Europe.

Sleet   Precipitation consisting mainly or entirely of ice pellets.

Snow pellet   An opaque, white pellet of compacted snow, less than one-fifth of an inch in diameter. Also called a graupel.

Snow roller   A barrel-shaped mass of snow formed when the wind causes snow that has melted slightly at its surface to roll down a slope.

Stationary front   A front whose forward motion has been stalled by a mountain range or the jet stream.

Stratocumulus   A low cloud consisting of an irregular layer of small cloudlets; formed when a stratus cloud breaks apart or when cumulus clouds come together at the same altitude.

Stratus   A low cloud in the form of a thick, gray, featureless layer, usually produced by condensation close to the ground. Stratus clouds may produce drizzle or light snow, but never the heavy precipitation of a nimbostratus or cumulonimbus.

Subtropical jet stream   One of two constant, eastward currents of air about eight miles above the ground, traveling at an average speed of about 100 miles per hour between 10 degrees and 30 degrees north and south of the Equator. *See also* **Westerly jet stream.**

Thermal   A current or column of air that is rising because it has been heated by the sun.

Thundercloud   *See* **Cumulonimbus.**

Tornado   A violent and rapidly spinning vortex of air that has been generated in a thunderstorm and touches the ground, where it causes extensive damage.

Trade winds   More or less constant winds that blow out of the northeast about 30 degrees north of the Equator, and out of the southeast at about 30 degrees south of the Equator.

Tropical depression   A cyclone formed over warm water near the Equator, larger and with more cloud cover than a tropical disturbance. The atmospheric pressure at the center of a tropical depression is low enough that one or more isobars are closed circles, but its winds are less than 40 miles per hour.

Tropical disturbance   A small, relatively weak cyclone formed over warm ocean water near the Equator.

Tropical storm   A tropical depression in which the wind is blowing at more than 39 miles an hour. A tropical storm represents the stage just before the development of a hurricane.

Trough   A zone of low atmospheric pressure lying beneath a southward bend in the westerly jet stream, where the wind is blowing cyclonically.

Typhoon   The name given to hurricanes in the Asian Pacific Ocean.

Valley fog Fog formed in a valley during an inversion, when cool moist air is trapped beneath a layer of warmer air above it; the moisture cannot escape, and a patch of fog develops.

Vertical clouds Clouds that form at any altitude from rising thermals of moist air. Cumulus and cumulonimbus are the principal vertical clouds.

Virga A light shower of rain that evaporates before reaching the ground.

Warm front The leading edge of a moving air mass that is warmer than the one it is replacing. Warm fronts usually travel more slowly than cold fronts, and are usually accompanied by precipitation that lasts longer.

Waterspout A rapidly spinning vortex generated in a thunderstorm, like a tornado, but touching the surface of the sea or a lake rather than the land.

Wave cloud See **Lenticular cloud.**

Weather vane A freely swinging device that is attached to a pole or other high place and shows the direction of the wind.

Westerly jet stream One of two constant, eastward currents of air about 8 miles above the ground, traveling at an average speed of about 100 miles per hour between 30 degrees and 50 degrees north and south of the Equator. *See also* **Subtropical jet stream.**

Willy-willy The name given to hurricanes in Australia.

Wind-chill factor The loss of heat from the skin caused by a combination of the temperature and the speed of the wind.

INDEX

Numbers in *italic* indicate illustrations.

PHOTO CREDITS

106—7: © Kevin Schafer

108: Courtesy NASA

110—11: © Nicholas Devore III/Photographers Aspen

113: © Neelon Crawford

114: (*top*) © Betty Crowell/Faraway Places; (*bottom*) © Kevin Schafer

115: (*both*) © Stewart Klipper

116—17: © Robert Holmes

118: (*top*) © Brad Fallin/Studio D; (*bottom*) © Betty Crowell/Faraway Places

119: © Philip Wallick

120: © Keith Kent

121: © Carl R. Sams, II/M.L. Dembinsky, Jr. Photography Associates

123: Arthur Rothstein/Collections of the Library of Congress

124—25: © Scott T. Smith

126: © Becky & Gary Vestal

127: © Robert Holmes

129: (*all*) Courtesy NASA

130: © Thomas R. Fletcher

131: (*both*) AP/Wide World Photos

132: © Warren Faidley/Weatherstock

133: © Tony Arruza

134: © Sylvia Schlender

136—37: © Chuck Place

139: (*top left*) © K. Brewster/Weatherstock; (*all others*) © Edi Ann Otto

140: © Laurence Parent

141: © Tony Arruza

142: © Fred Hirschmann

143: © Chlaus Lotscher

144—45: © Kevin Schafer

147: © Brad Fallin/Studio D

148—49: © John & Ann Mahan

150: © Warren Faidley/Weatherstock

151: © Robert Holmes

152: © John Messineo/Photographic Resources

153: © Keith Kent

154—55: © Sylvia Schlender

156—57: © Mary E. Messenger

158: © Tom Till

160, 161: Courtesy of the New York Historical Society, New York City

163: (*top*) Courtesy Johnstown Flood Museum; (*bottom*) AP/Wide World Photos

164—65: © Jeff Gnass

167: (*top*) © Thomas R. Fletcher; (*bottom*) © Paul Chesley/Photographers Aspen

168—69: © Mike Magnuson

170—71: © Kevin Schafer

173: © Paul Chesley/Photographers Aspen

174—75: © Jeff Gnass

176—78: © Fred Hirschmann

181: (*top*) © Sharon Cummings/M.L. Dembinsky, Jr. Photography Associates; (*bottom*) © Skip Moody/M.L. Dembinsky, Jr. Photography Associates

182—83: © Stan Osolinski/M.L. Dembinsky, Jr. Photography Associates

184—85: © Kevin Schafer

186—87: © Carol Simowitz

188: © Carl R. Sams, II/M.L. Dembinsky, Jr. Photography Associates

189: © Stan Osolinski/M.L. Dembinsky, Jr. Photography Associates

190: Collections of the Library of Congress

191: © Peter Guttman

192—93: © Sharon Cummings/M.L. Dembinsky, Jr. Photography Associates

194—99: © Peter Guttman

201: © Philip Wallick

202—205: © Tim Thompson

206—207: © Bruce Matheson

208, 210: © Tim Thompson

211: © Rod Planck/M.L. Dembinsky, Jr. Photography Associates

212: © Stan Osolinski/M.L. Dembinsky, Jr. Photography Associates

213: © Michael Longacre

214: Courtesy NASA

216—17: © David & Jan Couch/Photographics International

218: © Porterfield/Chickering

219—21: © Stan Osolinski/M.L. Dembinsky, Jr. Photography Associates

240: Collections of the Library of Congress

Designed by J.C. Suarés and Diana Jones

The text was composed in Futura Book by Trufont Typographers, Inc., Hicksville, New York.

The book was printed and bound by Dai Nippon Printing Company, Ltd., Tokyo, Japan.